CEMENT & CONCRETE PRODUCTS™

GUIDE TO CONCRETE

MASONRY & STUCCO PROJECTS

Creative Publishing
international

MINNEAPOLIS, MINNESOTA

www.creativepub.com

Creative Publishing international

Copyright © 2008
Creative Publishing international, Inc.
400 First Avenue North, Suite 300
Minneapolis, Minnesota 55401
1-800-328-3895
www.creativepub.com

Printed in China

10 9

Library of Congress Cataloging-in-Publication Data

Guide to concrete masonry & stucco projects.
    p. cm.
  At head of title: Quikrete.
  Includes index.
  Summary: "Includes common home repairs, as well as decorative and landscaping projects"--Provided by publisher.
  ISBN-13: 978-1-58923-416-1 (soft cover)
  ISBN-10: 1-58923-416-2 (soft cover)
  1. Concrete construction--Amateurs' manuals. 2. Stucco. 3. Dwellings--Maintenance and repair--Amateurs' manuals. 4. Landscape construction--Amateurs' manuals. I. Creative Publishing International.
II. Title: Guide to concrete masonry, and stucco projects.

TA682.42.G85 2008
693'.5--dc22

2008019919

QUIKRETE® Guide to Concrete Masonry & Stucco Projects
Created by: The editors of Creative Publishing international, Inc., in cooperation with QUIKRETE® International Inc.
QUIKRETE® is a trademark of QUIKRETE® International Inc.

President/CEO: Ken Fund

Home Improvement Group

Publisher: Bryan Trandem
Managing Editor: Tracy Stanley
Senior Editor: Mark Johanson
Editor: Jennifer Gehlhar

Creative Director: Michele Lanci-Altomare
Senior Design Managers: Jon Simpson, Brad Springer
Design Manager: James Kegley

Lead Photographer: Steve Galvin
Photo Coordinator: Joanne Wawra
Shop Manager: Bryan McLain
Shop Assistant: Cesar Fernandez Rodriguez

Production Managers: Linda Halls, Laura Hokkanen

Cover Design: Val Escher
Page Layout Artist: Val Escher
Photographers: Andrea Rugg, Joel Schnell
Shop Help: Livingston Allen, David Hartley

NOTICE TO READERS

For safety, use caution, care, and good judgment when following the procedures described in this book. The publisher and QUIKRETE® International Inc. cannot assume responsibility for any damage to property or injury to persons as a result of misuse of the information provided.

The techniques shown in this book are general techniques for various applications. In some instances, additional techniques not shown in this book may be required. Always follow manufacturers' instructions included with products, since deviating from the directions may void warranties. The projects in this book vary widely as to skill levels required: some may not be appropriate for all do-it-yourselfers, and some may require professional help.

Consult your local building department for information on building permits, codes, and other laws as they apply to your project.

CONTENTS QUIKRETE Guide to Concrete, Masonry & Stucco Projects

Introduction

Of all the building materials used in and around the home, few can match the quality and enduring beauty of concrete. Concrete, brick, stucco, and stone have long been prized for their timeless appeal and exceptional durability. Perhaps no other trade garners more respect than that of a skilled mason. Yet, with a little practice and the right products, you'll find that doing custom concrete and masonry work is easier than you think. Creating with concrete and masonry is not only a solid investment in a long-lasting material, it's also a great opportunity to learn unique skills that builders have used for centuries.

This book contains dozens of do-it-yourself projects that cover a wide range of materials and skill levels. Poured concrete takes center stage and is featured in everything from traditional applications, such as outdoor walkways, to contemporary favorites like kitchen countertops and interior floors. Indispensable for building foundations and garage slabs, concrete is equally suitable for fun, craft-sized projects like the garden borders.

For those who'd like to try their hand at the ancient art of bricklaying, there are several projects that focus on building with brick and concrete block. Like poured concrete, brick is at once structural and decorative. Concrete block is an inexpensive alternative to brick that offers similar strength and durability. Block can be left exposed, or finished with stucco or stone veneer—you'll learn how to install both finishes in these pages.

With each project you find in this book you'll also see a QUIK-DATA graphic that rates the relative cost of the projects as well as the amount of skill and time it requires. These estimates are made presuming a typical installation done by a DIYer with beginning to intermediate skills. Each category is rated from 1 dot (low) to 5 dots (high).

Walkways,
PATIOS & STEPS

Flat, level, and reassuringly solid, concrete is a natural underfoot. For walks and other outdoor surfaces, poured concrete offers exceptional durability and slip resistance along with a clean, finished appearance that stands up to decades of weathering. Indoors, concrete floors come with the same great durability but also a distinctive look and feel that you don't find with more conventional flooring materials. And you can enhance this look by applying an etching stain, instantly transforming a plain concrete floor into a one-of-a-kind-creation.

Building a new concrete walkway or set of steps is a good introduction to the basic techniques of flatwork, or horizontal concrete projects. First, you prepare the site with a base of compacted gravel, then you construct the form—the lumber mold that contains the wet concrete and defines the shape of the finished product. After the concrete is poured, or "placed," you strike it off level with the top of the form, then finish it with a trowel and other tools to give it just the right surface texture.

While the construction techniques for flatwork are simple and straightforward, the design possibilities are far from limited. This is because poured concrete will take the shape of almost any form you build. Graceful curves and artful shapes are really no more difficult to create than straight lines and squares. You can also color the concrete during mixing for an additional creative touch with professional quality results. Another option for a custom pathway or patio surface is the easiest of all: pouring the concrete right into a reusable plastic mold, which requires no form work and little, if any, site preparation.

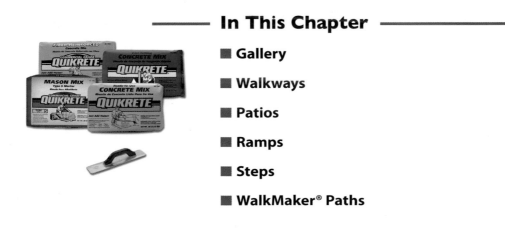

――――― In This Chapter ―――――

- ■ **Gallery**

- ■ **Walkways**

- ■ **Patios**

- ■ **Ramps**

- ■ **Steps**

- ■ **WalkMaker® Paths**

GALLERY Walkways, Patios & Steps

1 **Patio** Concrete floors and fireplace join forces to make a classic yet intimate conversation spot.

2 **Steps** Basic concrete entry steps are both practical and soothing as a neutral backdrop in landscapes.

3 **Walkways** Poured and stained concrete make up a geometric design element.

4 **Patios and Walkways** The versatility of concrete is obvious here, with stamped and colored concrete making up the unified patio and walkway system.

5 **Utility** For sheer practicality, nothing beats concrete. If you're just learning, start with small projects that can be poured in small sections. This walkway and utility area is really just a series of easy pouring projects set in a row.

TOOLS

Line level, hammer, shovel, sod cutter, wheelbarrow, tamper, drill, level, screed board, straightedge, mason's string, mason's float, mason's trowel, edger, groover, stiff-bristle broom.

MATERIALS

Garden stakes, rebar, bolsters, 2 × 4 lumber, 2½" and 3" screws, concrete mix or crack-resistant concrete mix, concrete sealer, isolation board, compactible gravel, construction adhesive, nails.

Walkways

Pouring a concrete walkway is one of the most practical projects you can master as a homeowner. Once you've excavated and poured a walkway, you can confidently take on larger concrete projects, such as patios and driveways.

Poured concrete sidewalls are practical and extremely durable. A frost footing is not required, but you will need to remove sod and excavate the site. The depth of the excavation varies from project to project and depends on the thickness of the concrete, plus the thickness of the sand or compactible gravel subbase. The subbase provides a more stable surface than the soil itself and an opportunity for water to run off so it does not pool directly under the walkway.

QUIK-TIP

Fiber-reinforced and air-entrained, crack-resistant concrete is recommended for concrete subjected to freezing and thawing to prevent scaling.

Tips for Building a Concrete Sidewalk

■ **Use a sod cutter** to strip grass from your pathway site. Available at most rental centers, sod cutters excavate to a very even depth. The cut sod can be replanted in other parts of your lawn.

■ **Install stakes and strings** when laying out straight walkways, and measure from the strings to ensure straight sides and uniform excavation depth.

Options for Directing Water off Walkways

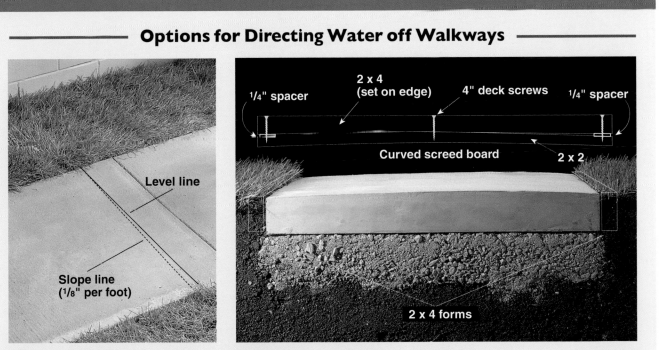

Level line

Slope line
(1/8" per foot)

1/4" spacer   2 x 4 (set on edge)   4" deck screws   1/4" spacer

Curved screed board   2 x 2

2 x 4 forms

■ **Slope walkways** away from the house to prevent water damage to the foundation or basement. Outline the location of the walkway with level mason's strings, then lower the outer string to create a slope of 1/8" per foot.

■ **Crown the walkway** so it is 1/4" higher at the center than at the edges. This will prevent water from pooling on the surface. To make the crown, construct a curved screed board by cutting a 2 × 2 and a 2 × 4 long enough to rest on the walkway forms. Butt them together edge to edge and insert a 1/4" spacer between them at each end. Attach the parts with 4" deck screws driven at the center and the edges. The 2 × 2 will be drawn up at the center, creating a curved edge. Screed the concrete with the curved edge of the screed board facing down.

How to Build a Concrete Sidewalk

1 ■ **Select a rough layout, including any turns.** Stake out the location and connect the stakes with mason's strings. Set the slope, if needed. Remove sod between and 6" beyond the lines, then excavate the site with a spade to a depth 4" greater than the thickness of the concrete walkway, following the slope lines to maintain consistent depth.

2 ■ **Pour a 5" layer** of compactible gravel as a subbase for the walkway. Tamp the subbase until it compacts to an even 4"- thick layer.

3 ■ **Build and install 2 × 4 forms set on edge**. Miter-cut the ends at angled joints. Position them so the inside edges are lined up with the strings. Attach the forms with 3" deck screws, then drive 2 × 4 stakes next to the forms at 3-ft. intervals. Attach the stakes to the forms with 2½" deck screws. Use a level to make sure forms are level or set to achieve the desired slope. Drive stakes at each side of angled joints.

4 ■ **Glue an isolation board** to the steps, house foundation, or other permanent structures that adjoin the walkway using construction adhesive.

5 ◼ **Prior to placing concrete,** it is necessary to dampen the gravel subbase. Spray the subbase using a water hose until saturated but do not leave standing water.

6 ◼ **Mix, then pour concrete** into the project area. Use a masonry hoe to spread it evenly within the forms.

7 ◼ **After pouring all of the concrete,** run a spade along the inside edges of the form, then rap the outside edges of the forms with a hammer to help settle the concrete.

continued next page ▶

Walkways, Patios & Steps ◼

8 ■ **Build a curved screed board** and use it to form a crown when you smooth out the concrete. Note: A helper makes this easier.

9 ■ **Smooth the concrete surface** with a wood float. The goal is to smooth it, not to level it (you should maintain the slight crown created by the curved screed board.

10 ■ **Shape the edges** of the concrete by running an edger along the forms. Smooth out any marks created by the edger using a float. Lift the leading edge of the edger and float slightly as you work.

11 ■ **Cut control joints** in the concrete after the concrete sets up but before it hardens.

— Control Joints —

■ Control joints are designed to allow for concrete expansion, contraction, and movement.

■ Control joints can be made using a grooving tool.

■ Control joints tell the concrete where to crack as it shrinks during the hardening process, which is called hydration.

■ Control joints made by a grooving tool must be a minimum of one-fourth the depth of the slab (for example, 1" deep for a 4"- thick slab).

■ Control joint spacing formula: Slab thickness (in inches) x 2.5 = joint placement interval (in feet). For example, 4" thick x 2.5 = 10 ft.

■ Keep the slab as square as possible.

12◼ Create a textured, nonskid surface by drawing a clean, stiff-bristled broom across the surface once the surface is thumbprint hard. Avoid overlapping broom marks.

13◼ Keep concrete damp by spraying periodically with a fine water mist or cover with plastic sheeting for five to seven days.

▶Option: Apply acrylic cure and seal with a garden sprayer or roller to eliminate the need for water curing and to seal the concrete for a more durable surface.

14◼ Remove the forms, then backfill the space at the sides of the walkway with dirt or sod. ◆

QUIK-DATA

Cost	● ● ●
Skill	● ● ●
Time	● ● ● ●

TOOLS

Rope, carpenter's square, hand maul, tape measure, mason's string, line level, spade, sod cutter, straightedge, level, wheelbarrow, shovel, hand tamper, circular saw, drill, paintbrush, concrete finishing tools, stiff-bristled broom.

MATERIALS

2 × 4 lumber, 3" screws, compactible gravel, vegetable oil or commercial release agent, concrete mix or crack-resistant concrete mix, acrylic cure & seal.

Patios

A poured concrete patio can be a gray, utilitarian slab or it may be a highly decorative focal point of your backyard living environment. By including a decorative finishing technique in your plans, such as exposed aggregates or etching with acid stain (see pages 112 to 113), your design options are virtually unlimited. A concrete patio also may serve as a subbase for a mortared flagstone, tile, or paver patio.

Building a concrete patio (or any concrete slab) is similar in many ways to the walkway project on the previous pages (10 to 15). Before beginning your project be sure and read through these pages for additional information, particularly on the subjects of finishing and curing. If your patio is larger than 10 ft. x 10 ft., you will definitely need to include control joints. You'll also want to consider buying or renting a power concrete mixer—see page 138 for a chart on estimating how many bags of concrete your patio will require.

QUIK-TIP

Contact your public utility company and have buried electric and gas lines marked before you begin to dig for this or any other project.

How to Prepare the Patio Site

1 ■ **Measure the slope** of the patio to determine if you need to do grading work before you start your project. First, drive stakes at each end of the project area. Attach a mason's string between the stakes and use a line level to set it at level. At each stake, measure from the string to the ground. The difference between the measurements (in inches) divided by the distance between stakes (in feet) will give you the slope (in inches per foot). If the slope is greater than 1" per foot, you may need to regrade the site.

2 ■ **Dig a test hole** to the planned depth so you can evaluate the soil conditions and get a better idea of how easy the excavation will be. Sandy or loose soil may require amending; consult a landscape engineer.

Shown cutaway

Compactible gravel subbase

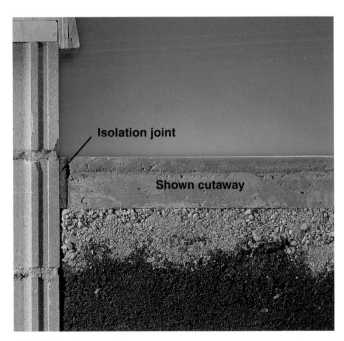

Isolation joint

Shown cutaway

3 ■ **Add a compactible gravel subbase** to provide a level, stable foundation for the concrete. The compactible gravel also improves drainage—an important consideration if you are building on soil that is high in clay content. For most building projects, pour a layer of compactible gravel about 5" thick, and use a tamper to compress it to 4".

4 ■ **When pouring concrete next to structures,** glue a ½"-thick piece of asphalt-impregnated fiber board to the adjoining structure to keep the concrete from bonding with the structure. The board creates an isolation joint, allowing the structures to move independently, minimizing the risk of damage. ◆

How to Lay Out & Excavate a Patio Site

1▪ Lay out a rough project outline with a rope or hose. Use a carpenter's square to set perpendicular lines. To create the actual layout, begin by driving wood stakes near each corner of the rough layout. The goal is to arrange the stakes so they are outside the actual project area, but in alignment with the borders of the project. Where possible, use two stakes set back 1 ft. from each corner, so strings intersect to mark each corner (below). Note: In projects built next to permanent structures, the structure will define one project side.

2▪ Connect the stakes with mason's strings. The strings should follow the actual project outlines. To make sure the strings are square, use the 3-4-5 triangle method (see page 149): measure and mark points 3 ft. out from one corner along one string, and 4 ft. out along the intersecting string at the corner. Measure between the points, and adjust the positions of the strings until the distance between the points is exactly 5 ft. A helper will make this easier.

3▪ Reset the stakes, if necessary, to conform to the positions of the squared strings. Check all corners with the 3-4-5 method, and adjust until the entire project area is exactly square. This can be a lengthy process with plenty of trial and error, but it is very important to the success of the project, especially if you plan to build on the concrete surface.

4▪ Attach a line level to one of the mason's strings to use as a reference. Adjust the string up or down as necessary until it is level. Adjust the other strings until they are level, making sure that intersecting strings contact one another (this ensures that they are all at the same height relative to ground level).

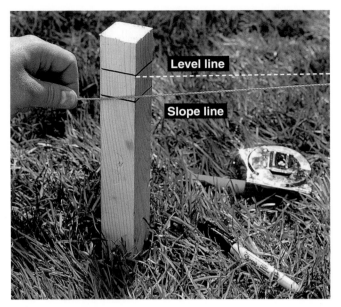

5■ To direct water runoff, most concrete surfaces should have a slight slope, especially if they are near your house. To create a slope, shift the level mason's strings on opposite sides of the project downward on their stakes (the lower end should be farther away from the house). To create a standard slope of ⅛" per ft., multiply the distance between the stakes on one side (in feet) by ⅛. For example, if the stakes were 10 ft. apart, the result would be ¹⁰⁄₈ (1¼"). You would move the strings down 1¼" on the stakes on the low ends.

6■ Start excavating by removing the sod. Use a sod cutter if you wish to reuse the sod elsewhere in your yard (lay the sod as soon as possible). Otherwise, use a square-end spade to cut away sod. Strip off the sod at least 6" beyond the mason's strings. The subbase should extend at least 6" beyond the project area. You may need to remove the strings temporarily for this step.

7■ Make a story pole as a guide for excavating the site. First, measure down to ground level from the high end of a slope line. Add 7½" to that distance (4" for the subbase material and 3½" for the concrete if you are using 2 × 4 forms). Mark the total distance on the story pole, measuring from one end. Remove soil from the site with a spade. Use the story pole to make sure the bottom of the site is consistent (the same distance from the slope line at all points) as you dig. Check points at the center of the site using a straightedge and a level placed on top of the soil.

8■ Lay a subbase for the project (unless it requires a frost footing). Pour a 5"-thick layer of gravel, and tamp until the gravel is even and compressed to 4" in depth. ◆

How to Build & Install Patio Forms

1 ■ **A form is a frame,** usually made from 2 × 4 lumber, laid around a project site to contain poured concrete and establish its thickness. Cut 2 × 4s to create a frame with inside dimensions equal to the total size of the project.

2 ■ **Use the mason's strings** that outline the project as a reference for setting form boards in place. Starting with the longest form board, position the boards so the inside edges are directly below the strings.

3 ■ **Cut several pieces** of 2 × 4 at least 12" long to use as stakes. Trim one end of each stake to a sharp point. Drive the stakes at 3-ft. intervals at the outside edges of the form boards, positioned to support any joints in the form boards.

4 ■ **Drive 3" Deck Screws** through the stakes and into the form board on one side. Set a level so it spans the staked side of the form and the opposite form board, and use the level as a guide as you stake the second form board so it is level with the first. For large projects, use the mason's strings as the primary guide for setting the height of all form boards.

5 ■ **Once the forms are staked and leveled,** drive 3" deck screws at the corners. Coat the insides of the forms with vegetable oil or a commercial release agent so concrete won't bond to them. *Tip: Tack nails to the outsides of the forms to mark locations for control joints. See page 14 for joint placement recommendations.*

How to Pour & Finish a Patio

1■ **Install reinforcement (optional)** such as rebar and rewire set on bolsters (inset photo), and then mix and pour the concrete (see pages 12 to 15 and 138 to 143). The use of fiber-reinforced crack-resistant concrete eliminates the need for wire reinforcing mesh.

2■ **Screed concrete** level with the forms. Use a 2 x 4 in a sawing motion to level and remove excess concrete.

3■ **Float the concrete surface** to create a surface that is both smooth and skid resistant. Wait until bleed water has disappeared before proceeding. Finish options include a broomed finish, a smooth steel-trowel finish or seed with small aggregate after floating.

4■ **Cut control joints** in larger patios. Lay a 2 x 4 straightedge guide on the surface and carefully tool control joints using a grooving tool. Allow the concrete to dry until sheen disappears, and then treat with acrylic cure and seal (see page 15). ◆

Concrete is a great material for small ramps. It's strong enough to support heavy equipment and can be made with a nonslip surface for sure footing in wet weather.

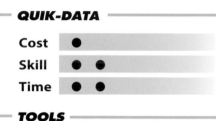

QUIK-DATA

Cost	●
Skill	● ●
Time	● ●

TOOLS

Form-building tools, concrete mixing tools, shovel, concrete float, concrete edger, fine-bristled broom or wood concrete float.

MATERIALS

Compactible gravel, ¾" exterior-grade plywood, 2 x 4 lumber, wood screws, stakes, isolation board (if required), vegetable oil or form release agent, concrete mix.

Ramps

A simple concrete ramp can be the perfect solution for moving heavy equipment in and out of a backyard shed or for easing the transition between a walkway and a raised patio, driveway, or stoop. Constructing a ramp is much like building a poured concrete walkway or a small slab: you build a wood form over a compacted gravel base, then place the concrete, and finish the surface so it's level with the top of the form. To create the slope of the ramp, build the sides of the form with pieces of plywood cut at an angle along the top.

The key to shaping the concrete into a slope is to use a stiff mixture; if the concrete is too wet, it will slump down to the bottom of the ramp, seeking its own level. As you fill the form, flatten and smooth the concrete with a float, working from the bottom up. Determining the length of the ramp—and thus the slope—is up to you (the longer the ramp, the gentler the slope). However, if you're building the ramp for wheelchair access, make sure its dimensions, slope, and nonslip finish meet the requirements of the local building code.

Estimating Concrete for Your Project

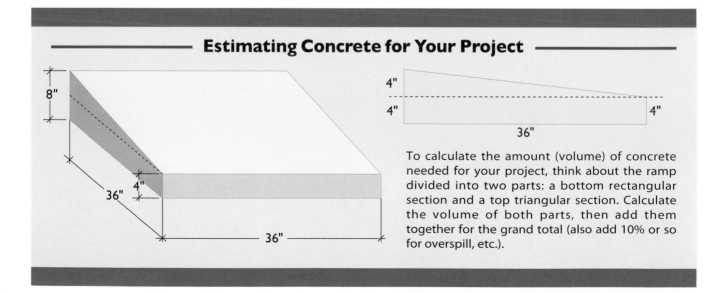

To calculate the amount (volume) of concrete needed for your project, think about the ramp divided into two parts: a bottom rectangular section and a top triangular section. Calculate the volume of both parts, then add them together for the grand total (also add 10% or so for overspill, etc.).

How to Build a Concrete Ramp

1 ■ **Prepare a subbase for the ramp** with 4" of compacted gravel. Build the ramp form using ¾" plywood and 2 x 4 lumber. Make sure the side pieces are identical and will sit level with each other across the top.

2 ■ **Stake and brace the form securely,** checking it for level. If either end of the ramp will meet a walkway, slab, or other permanent structure, attach a piece of isolation board at the juncture.

3 ■ **Mix the concrete so it's just wet enough** to be workable. Fill the form, and use a float to pat and smooth the concrete as you go, working from the bottom up. Use a shovel to settle the concrete as you place it, and rap the form sides to help create a smooth finish on the sides of the ramp.

4 ■ **Round over the edges of the ramp** using an edger. Texture the ramp surface for slip resistance by brooming it or using a wood float for the final finishing. Moist cure the concrete for five to seven days. The form can be removed after three days. ◆

Steps

Designing steps requires some calculations and some trial and error. As long as the design meets safety guidelines, you can adjust elements such as the landing depth and the dimensions of the steps. Sketching your plan on paper will make the job easier.

Before demolishing your old steps, measure them to see if they meet safety guidelines. If so, you can use them as a reference for your new steps. If not, start from scratch so your new steps do not repeat any design errors.

For steps with more than two risers, you'll need to install a handrail. Ask a building inspector about other requirements.

QUIK-DATA

Cost	● ●
Skill	● ● ● ●
Time	● ● ●

TOOLS

Tape measure, sledge hammer, shovel, drill, reciprocating saw, level, mason's string, hand tamper, mallet, concrete mixing tools, jigsaw, clamps, ruler or framing square, float, step edger, stiff- bristled broom.

MATERIALS

concrete mix or crack resistant concrete mix, 2 × 4 lumber, steel rebar grid, wire, bolsters, construction adhesive, compactible gravel, fill material, exterior-grade ¾" plywood, 2" deck screws, isolation board, #3 rebar, stakes, latex caulk, vegetable oil or commercial release agent, acrylic cure & seal.

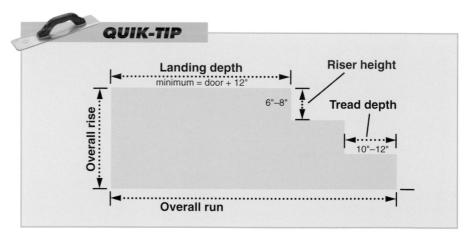

QUIK-TIP

Landing depth
minimum = door + 12"

Riser height

6"–8"

Tread depth

10"–12"

Overall rise

Overall run

How to Design Steps

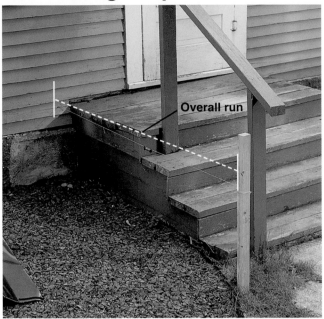

1 ■ **Attach a mason's string** to the house foundation, 1" below the bottom of the door threshold. Drive a stake where you want the base of the bottom step to fall. Attach the other end of the string to the stake and use a line level to level it. Measure the length of the string—this distance is the overall depth, or run, of the steps.

2 ■ **Measure down from the string** to the bottom of the stake to determine the overall height, or rise, of the steps. Divide the overall rise by the estimated number of steps. The rise of each step should be between 6" and 8". For example, if the overall rise is 21" and you plan to build three steps, the rise of each step would be 7" (21 divided by 3), which falls within the recommended safety range for riser height.

3 ■ **Measure the width** of your door and add at least 12"; this number is the minimum depth you should plan for the landing area of the steps. The landing depth plus the depth of each step should fit within the overall run of the steps. If necessary, you can increase the overall run by moving the stake at the planned base of the steps away from the house, or by increasing the depth of the landing.

4 ■ **Sketch a detailed plan for the steps**, keeping these guidelines in mind: each step should be 10" to 12" deep, with a riser height between 6" and 8", and the landing should be at least 12" deeper than the swing radius (width) of your door. Adjust the parts of the steps as needed, but stay within the given ranges. Creating a final sketch will take time, but it is worth doing carefully. ◆

How to Build Concrete Steps

1■ **Remove or demolish existing steps;** if the old steps are concrete, set aside the rubble to use as fill material for the new steps. Wear protective gear, including eye protection and gloves, when demolishing concrete.

2■ **Dig 12"-wide trenches** to the required depth for footings. Locate the trenches perpendicular to the foundation, spaced so the footings will extend 3" beyond the outside edges of the steps. Install steel rebar grids for reinforcement. Affix isolation boards to the foundation wall inside each trench using a few dabs of construction adhesive.

3■ **Mix the concrete** and pour the footings. Level and smooth the concrete with a screed board. You do not need to float the surface afterwards.

4■ **When bleed water** disappears, insert 12" sections of rebar 6" into the concrete, spaced at 12" intervals and centered side to side. Leave 1 ft. of clear space at each end.

5■ **Let the footings cure** for two days, then excavate the area between them to 4" deep. Pour in a 5"-thick layer of compactible gravel subbase and tamp until it is level with the footings.

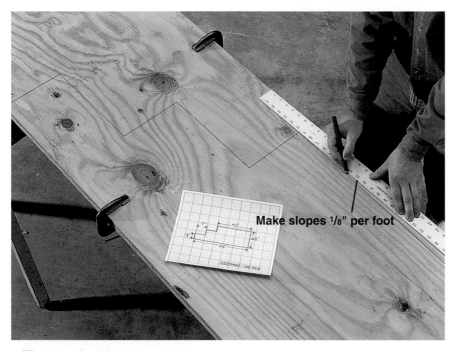

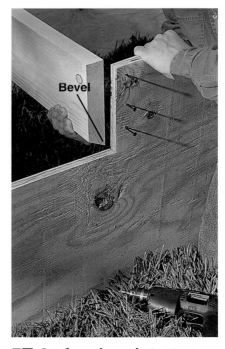

6 ■ **Transfer the measurements** for the side forms from your working sketch onto ¾" exterior-grade plywood. Cut out the forms along the cutting lines using a jigsaw. Save time by clamping two pieces of plywood together and cutting both side forms at the same time. Add a ⅛" per foot back-to-front slope to the landing part of the form.

7 ■ **Cut form boards** for the risers to fit between the side forms. Bevel the bottom edges of the boards when cutting to create clearance for the float at the back edges of the steps. Attach the riser forms to the side forms with 2" deck screws.

8 ■ **Cut a 2 × 4 to make a center support** for the riser forms. Use 2" deck screws to attach 2 × 4 cleats to the riser forms, then attach the support to the cleats. Check to make sure all corners are square.

9 ■ **Cut an isolation board and glue it** to the house foundation at the back of the project area. Set the form onto the footings, flush against the isolation board. Add 2 × 4 bracing arms to the sides of the form, attaching them to cleats on the sides and to stakes driven into the ground.

continued next page ▶

10 ■ **Fill the form with clean fill** (broken concrete or rubble). Stack the fill carefully, keeping it 6" away from the sides, back, and top edges of the form. Shovel smaller fragments onto the pile to fill the void areas.

11 ■ **Lay pieces of #3 metal rebar on top** of the fill at 12" intervals, and attach them to bolsters with wire to keep them from moving when the concrete is poured. Keep rebar at least 2" below the top of the forms. Mist the forms and the rubble with water.

12 ■ **Coat the forms** with vegetable oil or a commercial release agent, then mist them with water so concrete won't stick to the forms. Mix concrete and pour steps one at a time, beginning at the bottom. Settle and smooth the concrete with a screed board. Press a piece of #3 rebar 2" down into the "nose" of each tread for reinforcement.

13 ■ **Float the steps,** working the front edge of the float underneath the beveled edge at the bottom of each riser form.

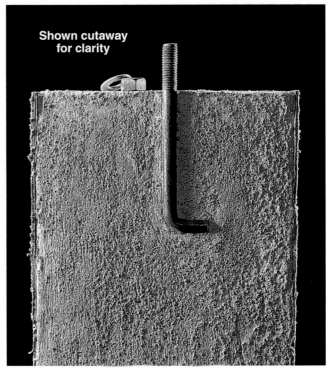

14 **Pour concrete into the forms** for the remaining steps and the landing. Press rebar into the nose of each step. Keep an eye on the poured concrete as you work, and stop to float any concrete as soon as the bleed water disappears.

▶ **Option:** For railings with mounting plates that attach to sunken J-bolts, install the bolts before the concrete sets. Use anchoring cement to set bolts in previously drilled holes in concrete.

15 **Once the concrete sets,** shape the steps and landing with a step edger. Float the surface. Sweep with a stiff-bristled broom for maximum traction.

16 **Remove the forms** as soon as the surface is firm to the touch, usually within several hours. Smooth rough edges with a float. Add concrete to fill any holes. If forms are removed later, more patching may be required. Backfill the area around the base of the steps, and seal the concrete. Install a railing. ◆

Basket Weave Brick

Country Stone Pattern

Running Bond Brick

European Block Brick

Walkmaker® molds are available in four decorative patterns, shown here: Basket Weave Brick, Running Bond Brick, Country Stone, and European Block Brick.

Walkmaker® Paths

A well-made walkway or garden path not only stands up to years of hard use, it enhances the natural landscape and complements a home's exterior features. While traditional walkway materials like brick and stone have always been prized for both appearance and durability, most varieties are quite pricey and often difficult to install. As an easy and inexpensive alternative, you can build a new concrete path using manufactured forms. The result is a beautiful pathway that combines the custom look of brick or natural stone with all the durability and economy of poured concrete.

Building a path is a great do-it-yourself project. Once you've laid out the path, you mix the concrete, set and fill the form, then lift off the form to reveal the finished design. After a little troweling to smooth the surfaces, you're ready to create the next section—using the same form. Simply repeat the process until the path is complete. Each form creates a section that's approximately 2-ft. sq. using one 80-lb. bag of premixed concrete. This project shows you all the basic steps for making any length of pathway, plus special techniques for making curves, adding a custom finish, or coloring the concrete to suit your personal design.

TOOLS

Excavation and site preparation tools, QUIKRETE® Walkmaker form, wheelbarrow or mixing box, shovel, level, margin trowel or finishing trowel.

MATERIALS

Concrete mix or crack-resistant concrete mix, liquid cement color, plastic sheeting, polymer-modified jointing sand.

Estimating Concrete for Your Project

For Basket Weave Brick, Running Bond Brick, and European Block Brick patterns:

Length of walk	# of Poured Sections	# of 80-lb. Bags of Concrete	# of 60-lb. Bags of Concrete
2 ft.	1	1	2
4 ft.	2	2	3
6 ft.	3	3	4
10 ft.	5	5	7
16 ft.	8	8	11
24 ft.	12	12	16
30 ft.	15	15	20

For Country Stone Pattern (interlocks so each section is approx. 1 ft. 9 in.):

Length of walk	# of Poured Sections	# of 80-lb. Bags of Concrete	# of 60-lb. Bags of Concrete
2 ft.	1	1	2
3 ft. 9 in.	2	2	3
5 ft. 6 in.	3	3	4
9 ft.	5	5	7
16 ft.	9	9	12
23 ft.	13	13	18
30 ft.	17	17	23

How to Create a Walkmaker® Path

1 ■ **Prepare the project site** by leveling the ground, removing sod or soil as needed. For a more durable base, excavate the area and add 2 to 4" of compactible gravel. Grade and compact the gravel layer so it is level and flat.

2 ■ **Mix a batch of concrete** for the first section, following the product directions (see page 33 to add color, as we have done here). Place the form at the start of your path and level it, if desired. Shovel the wet concrete into the form to fill each cavity. Consolidate and smooth the surface of the form using a concrete margin trowel.

3 ■ **Promptly remove the form,** and then trowel the edges of the section to create the desired finish (it may help to wet the trowel in water). For a nonslip surface, broom the section or brush it with a stiff brush. Place the form against the finished section and repeat steps 2 and 3 to complete the next section. Forms can be rotated to vary pattern.

4 ■ **After removing each form,** remember to trowel the edges of the section to create the desired finish. Repeat until the path is finished. If desired, rotate the form 90° with each section to vary the pattern. Damp-cure the entire path for five to seven days. ◆

How to Create a Curved Walkway with Faux Mortar Joints

1 ■ **After removing the form from a freshly poured section, reposition the form** in the direction of the curve and press down to slice off the inside corner of the section (photo left). Trowel the cut edge (and rest of the section) to finish. Pour the next section following the curve (photo right). Cut off as many sections as needed to complete the curve.

2 ■ **Sprinkle the area** around the joint or joints between pavers with polymer-modified jointing sand after the concrete has cured sufficiently so that the sand does not adhere. Sweep the product into the gap to clean the paver surfaces while filling the gap.

3 ■ **Next, simply mist** the jointing sand with clean water, taking care not to wash the sand out of the joint. Once the water dries, the polymers in the mixture will have hardened the sand to look like a mortar joint. Refresh as needed. ◆

 **QUIK-TIP**

Use QUIKRETE® PowerLoc jointing sand in place of play sand to simulate mortar joints. Sweep the polymer-modified sand into the joints, mist with water, and Powerloc will harden in place.

Coloring Your Concrete Path

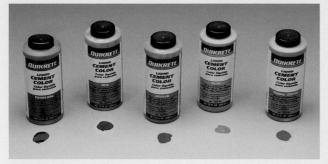

Coloring gives molded concrete a more natural-looking finish and is great for blending your path or walkway into your landscape design. Adding colorant to the concrete mix is the easiest method and produces consistent results:

1 For every two 60-lb. or 80-lb. bags of dry concrete mix, first blend one 10 ounce bottle of QUIKRETE® liquid cement color with 5 quarts of clean water. Mix the liquid into the dry concrete until the color is uniform. Add more clean water as needed to achieve the desired consistency.

2 After placing and finishing the path sections, cure the concrete carefully to produce the best color quality. If curing conditions will be less than ideal, apply QUIKRETE® concrete sealer to ensure slow, even curing and good coloring.

▶ Adding Decorative Effects

■ **Fill walkway joints** with sand or mortar mix to mimic the look of hand-laid stone or brick. Sweep the sand or dry mortar into the section contours and spaces between sections. For mortar, mist the joints with water so they harden in place.

■ **Create custom surface finishes** by pressing small stones or pea gravel into the wet concrete or by brushing on a layer of sand. Apply finish materials after the concrete has reached its initial set (thumb print hard) but is still damp—approximately one hour after placing.

Outdoor Home
& LANDSCAPING

Concrete and masonry have always played a special role in the home landscape. In contrast to the ready-made look of a portable grill or seasonal lawn furniture, a built-in brick barbecue or a concrete garden bench adds a sense of craftsmanship and permanence to an outdoor setting. On the structural side of things, ordinary landscape features like fences, lampposts, and play equipment are safer and longer-lasting when set into the ground with concrete.

In keeping with the many uses for concrete and masonry in the outdoor home, the projects in this section cover a range of applications, from custom-crafted garden border blocks to structural deck footings that are required by most building codes. The projects also include a range of concrete and masonry building techniques. For example, the concrete bench and garden borders teach you the basics of mold-casting with concrete, while the barbecue involves concrete foundation work as well as traditional brick wall construction.

The outdoor kitchen is the most ambitious project of the group and lets you try your hand at several building techniques, including laying up concrete block, applying a stucco finish, and crafting a poured-in-place concrete countertop. You'll also find complete instructions for building a mold-cast concrete countertop, perfect for an outdoor work surface or as a countertop anywhere outside or inside the home. For additional ideas on outdoor home and landscape projects, browse through the masonry wall projects in the next section, "Walls & Wall Finishes."

In This Chapter

- **Gallery**

- **Outdoor Kitchen**

- **Brick Barbecue**

- **Concrete Landscape & Garden Borders**

- **Pouring Posts in Footings**

GALLERY **Outdoor Home & Landscaping**

1 ■ **Kitchen** Outdoor kitchen workstations and concrete/masonry products are a great pairing. A stucco finish over a stacked block grilling center lasts a long time and blends beautifully with a tile countertop.

2 ■ **Fireplace** Outdoor fireplaces fashioned from masonry products are becoming common backyard entertaining elements. They often resemble indoor fireplaces to a much greater extent than they look like fire pits or barbecues.

3 ■ **Brick barbecue** Poured concrete slab and mortared brick walls create a legacy-style outdoor cooking area.

4 ■ **Borders** Landscape borders define space while serving the practical purpose of preventing landscape materials from integrating. Some borders are also designed to be mowing borders that can support the wheels of your lawn mower.

5 ■ **Molded borders** Poured concrete in homemade forms creates a unique garden border treatment.

Outdoor Kitchen

TOOLS

Chalk line, pointed trowel, masonry mixing tools, level, mason's string, circular saw with masonry blade, utility knife, straightedge, square-notched trowel, metal snips, wood float, steel finishing trowel, drill with masonry bit, concrete block.

MATERIALS

Mortar mix or mason mix, metal reinforcement (as required), steel angle iron, ½" cementboard (two 8-ft.-long sheets), 2 x 4 and 2 x 6 lumber, 2½ and 3" deck screws, galvanized metal stucco lath, silicone caulk, vegetable oil or other release agent, countertop concrete mix or QUIKRETE® 5000, base coat stucco, finish coat stucco.

With its perfect blend of indoor convenience and alfresco atmosphere, it's easy to see why the outdoor kitchen is one of today's most popular home upgrades. In terms of design, outdoor kitchens can take almost any form, but most are planned around the essential elements of a built-in grill and convenient countertop surfaces (preferably on both sides of the grill). Secure storage inside the cooking cabinet is another feature many outdoor cooks find indispensable.

The kitchen design in this project combines all three of these elements in a moderately sized cooking station that can fit a variety of kitchen configurations. The structure is freestanding and self-supporting, so it can go almost anywhere—on top of a patio, right next to a house wall, out by the pool, or out in the yard to create a remote entertainment getaway. Adding a table and chairs or a casual sitting area might be all you need to complete your kitchen accommodations. But best of all, this kitchen is made almost entirely of inexpensive masonry materials.

Concrete and masonry are ideally suited to outdoor kitchen construction. It's noncombustible, not damaged by water, and can easily withstand decades of outdoor exposure. In fact, a little weathering makes masonry look even better. In this project, the kitchen's structural cabinet is built with concrete block on top of a reinforced concrete slab. The countertop is 2"-thick poured concrete that you cast in place over two layers of cementboard (for a small kitchen or a standalone island, you might prefer to build a mold-cast countertop; see page 98). The block sides of the cabinet provide plenty of support for the countertop, as well as a good surface for applying the stucco finish. You could also finish the cabinet with veneer stone or tile.

►Construction Details

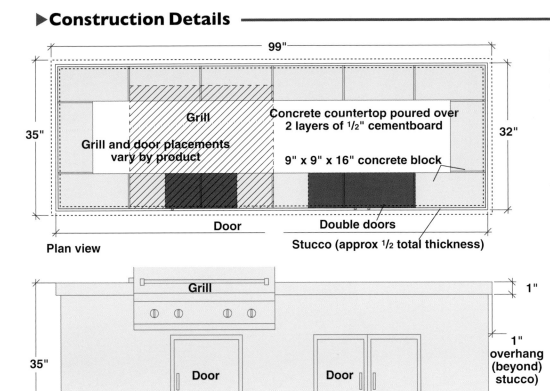

99"

35"

Grill

Grill and door placements vary by product

Concrete countertop poured over 2 layers of ½" cementboard

9" x 9" x 16" concrete block

32"

Door

Double doors

Stucco (approx ½ total thickness)

Plan view

Grill

35"

Door

Door

1"

1" overhang (beyond) stucco

Front elevation

Concrete slab (reinforced as required)

■ **The basic structure** of this kitchen consists of five courses of standard 8" x 8" x 16" concrete block. Two mortared layers of ½" cementboard serve as a base for the countertop. The 2"-thick poured concrete layer of the countertop extends 1½" beyond the rough block walls and covers the cementboard edges. The walls receive a two-coat stucco finish, which can be tinted during the mixing or painted after it cures. Doors in the front of the cabinet provide access to storage space inside and to any utility connections for the grill. The kitchen's dimensions can easily be adjusted to accommodate a specific location, cooking equipment, or doors and additional amenities.

Planning a Kitchen Project

Whether you model your project after the one shown here or create your own design, there are a few critical factors to address as part of your initial planning:

■ **Foundation** Check with your local building department about foundation requirements for your kitchen. Depending on the kitchen's size and location, you may be allowed to build on top of a standard 4"-thick reinforced concrete patio slab, or you might need frost footings or a reinforced "floating footing" similar to the one shown on page 47 (Brick Barbecue).

■ **Grill & Door Units** You'll need the exact dimensions of the grill, doors, and any other built-in features before you draw up your plans and start building. When shopping for equipment, keep in mind its utility requirements and the type of support system needed for the grill and other large units. Some grills are drop-in and are supported only by the countertop; others must be supported below with a noncombustible, load-bearing material such as concrete block or a poured concrete platform.

■ **Utility Hookups** Grills fueled by natural gas require a plumbed gas line, and those with electric starters need an outdoor electrical circuit, both

A grill gas line typically extends up into the cabinet space under the grill and is fitted with a shutoff valve.

running into the kitchen cabinet. To include a kitchen sink, you'll need a dedicated water line and a drain connection (to the house system, directly to the city sewer, or possibly to a dry well on your property). Outdoor utilities are strictly governed by building codes, so check with the building department for requirements. Generally, the rough-in work for utilities is best left to professionals.

continued next page ▶

1 ■ **Pour the foundation or prepare the slab** for the wall construction. See pages 58 to 61 for help with building frost footings and pages 140 to 143 for pouring a concrete slab. To prepare an existing slab, clean the surface thoroughly to remove all dirt, oils, concrete sealers, and paint that could prevent a good bond with mortar.

2 ■ **Dry-lay the first course of block** on the foundation to test the layout. If desired, use 2- or 4"-thick solid blocks under the door openings. Snap chalk lines to guide the block installation, and mark the exact locations of the door openings.

3 ■ **Set the first course of block into mortar**, following the basic techniques shown on pages 84 to 87. Cut blocks as needed for the door openings. Lay the second course, offsetting the joints with the first course in a running bond pattern.

4 ■ **Continue laying up the wall**, adding reinforcing wire or rebar if required by local building code. Instead of tooling the mortar joints for a concave profile, use a trowel to slice excess mortar from the blocks. This creates a flat surface that's easier to cover with stucco.

5■ **Install steel angle lintels** to span over the door openings. If an opening is in line with a course of block, mortar the lintels in place on top of the block. Otherwise, use a circular saw with a masonry blade to cut channels for the horizontal leg of the angle. Lintels should span 6" beyond each side of an opening. Slip the lintel into the channels, and then fill the block cells containing the lintel with mortar to secure the lintel in place. Lay a bed of mortar on top of the lintels, then set block into the mortar. Complete the final course of block in the cabinet and let the mortar cure.

6■ **Cut two 8-ft.-long sheets of cementboard** to match the outer dimensions of the block cabinet. Apply mortar to the tops of the cabinet blocks and then set one layer of cementboard into the mortar. If you will be installing a built-in grill or other accessories, make cutouts in the cementboard with a utility knife or a jigsaw with a remodeler's blade.

7■ **Cut pieces to fit** for a second layer of cementboard. Apply a bed of mortar to the top of the first panel, and then lay the second layer pieces on top, pressing them into the mortar so the surfaces are level. Let the mortar cure.

continued next page ▶

8 ▪ To create a 1½" overhang for the countertop, build a perimeter band of 2 x 4 lumber; this will serve as the base of the concrete form. Cut the pieces to fit tightly around the cabinet along the top. Fasten the pieces together at their ends with 3" screws so their top edges are flush with the bottom of the cementboard.

9 ▪ Cut vertical 2 x 4 supports to fit snugly between the foundation and the bottom of the 2 x 4 band. Install a support at the ends of each wall and evenly spaced in between. Secure each support with angled screws driven into the band boards.

10 ▪ Build the sides of the countertop form with 2 x 6s cut to fit around the 2 x 4 band. Position the 2 x 6s so their top edges are 2" above the cementboard, and fasten them to the band with 2 ½" screws.

11 ▪ Form the opening for the grill using 2 x 6 side pieces (no overhang inside opening). Support the edges of the cementboard along the grill cutout with cleats attached to the 2 x 6s. Add vertical supports as needed under the cutout to keep the form from shifting under the weight of the concrete.

12 ◼ **Cut a sheet of stucco lath** to fit into the countertop form, leaving a 2" space along the inside perimeter of the form. Remove the lath and set it aside. Seal the form joints with a fine bead of silicone caulk and smooth with a finger. After the caulk dries, coat the form boards (not the cementboard) with vegetable oil or other release agent.

13 ◼ **Dampen the cementboard** with a mist of water. Mix a batch of countertop mix, adding color if desired (see page 33). Working quickly, fill along the edges of the form with concrete, carefully packing it down into the overhang portion by hand.

14 ◼ **Fill the rest of the form** halfway up with an even layer of concrete. Lay the stucco lath on top then press it lightly into the concrete with a float. Add the remaining concrete so it's flush with the tops of the 2 x 6s.

15 ◼ **Tap along the outsides of the form** with a hammer to remove air bubbles trapped against the inside edges. Screed the top of the concrete with a straight 2 x 4 riding along the form sides. Add concrete as needed to fill in low spots so the surface is perfectly flat.

continued next page ▶

16■ **After the bleed water disappears**, float the concrete with a wood or magnesium float. The floated surface should be flat and smooth but will still have a somewhat rough texture. Be careful not to overfloat and draw water to the surface.

17■ **A few hours after floating,** finish the countertop as desired. A few passes with a steel finishing trowel yields the smoothest surface. Hold the leading edge of the trowel up and work in circular strokes. Let the concrete set for a while between passes.

18■ **Moist-cure the countertop** with a fine water mist for three to five days. Remove the form boards. If desired, smooth the countertop edges with an abrasive brick and/or a diamond pad or sandpaper. After the concrete cures, apply a food-safe sealer to help prevent staining.

19■ **Prepare for door installation in the cabinet.** Outdoor cabinet doors are usually made of stainless steel, and typically are installed by hanging hinges or flanges with masonry anchors. Drill holes for masonry anchors in the concrete block, following the door manufacturer's instructions.

QUIK-TIP

Honeycombs or air voids can be filled using a cement slurry of cement and water applied with a rubber float. If liquid cement color was used in your countertop concrete mix, color should be added to the wet cement paste. Some experimentation will be necessary.

20■ **Finish installing** and hanging the doors. Test the door operations and make sure to caulk around the edges with high-quality silicone caulk. NOTE: Doors shown here are best installed before the stucco finish is applied to the cabinet. Other doors may be easier to install following a different sequence.

21 ▇ To finish the cabinet walls, begin by dampening the concrete block and then applying a ⅜"-thick base coat of stucco, following the steps on pages 70 to 75. Apply an even layer over the walls; then smooth the surface with a wood float and moist-cure the stucco for 48 hours or as directed by the manufacturer.

22 ▇ Apply a finish coat of tinted stucco that's at least ⅛" thick. Evenly saturate the base coat stucco surface with water prior to applying the the finish coat. Texture the surface as desired. Moist-cure the stucco for several days as directed.

23 ▇ Set the grill into place, make the gas connection, then check it carefully for leaks. Permanently install the grill following the manufacturer's directions. The joints around grills are highly susceptible to water intrusion; seal them thoroughly with an approved caulk to help keep moisture out of the cabinet space below. ◆

Brick Barbecue

The barbecue design shown here is constructed with double walls—an inner wall, made of heat-resistant fire brick set on edge, surrounding the cooking area, and an outer wall, made of engineer brick. We chose this brick because its larger dimensions mean you'll have fewer bricks to lay. You'll need to adjust the design if you select another brick size. A 4" air space between the walls helps insulate the cooking area. The walls are capped with thin pieces of cut stone.

Refractory mortar is recommended for use in areas of direct fire contact. It is heat resistant and the joints will last a long time without cracking. Ask a local brick yard to recommend a refractory mortar for outdoor use.

The foundation combines a 12"-deep footing supporting a reinforced slab. This structure, known as a floating footing, is designed to shift as a unit when temperature changes cause the ground to shift. Ask a building inspector about local Building Code specifications.

QUIK-DATA

Cost	● ●
Skill	● ● ● ●
Time	● ● ●

TOOLS

Tape measure, hammer, brickset chisel, mason's string, shovel, aviation snips, reciprocating saw or hacksaw, masonry hoe, shovel, wood float, chalk line, level, wheelbarrow, mason's trowel, jointing tool.

MATERIALS

Garden stakes, 2 × 4 lumber, 18-gauge galvanized metal mesh, #4 rebar, 16-gauge tie wire, bolsters, fire brick (4½ × 2½ × 9"), engineer brick (4 × 3¹/₅ × 8"), Type N or Type S mortar, ³/₈"-dia. dowel, metal ties, 4" tee plates, engineer brick (4 × 2 × 12"), brick sealer, stainless steel expanded mesh (23¾ × 30"), cooking grills (23⁵/₈ × 15½"), ash pan, concrete mix.

Mortar Data

Type N Mortar: Non-structural mortar for veneer applications, reaches 750 psi @ 28 days

Type S Mortar: Structural mortar for veneer structural applications, exceeds 1,800 psi @ 28 days

Pouring a Floating Footing

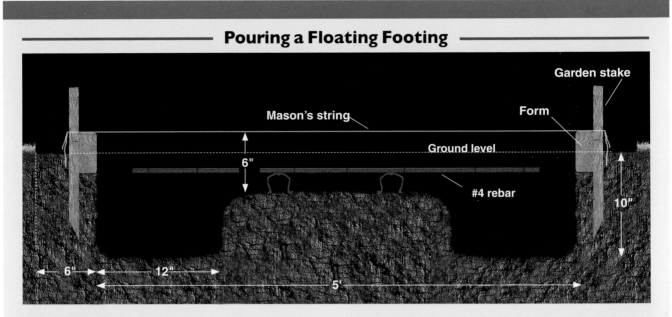

▶**Lay out a 4 × 5-ft. area.** Dig a continuous trench 12" wide × 10" deep along the perimeter of the area, leaving a rectangular mound in the center. Remove 4" of soil from the top of the mound, and round over the edges. Set a 2 × 4 form around the site so that the top is 2" above the ground along the back and 1½" above the ground along the front. This slope will help shed water.

Reinforce the footing with five 52"-long pieces of rebar. Use a mason's string and a line level to ensure that the forms are level from side to side. Set the rebar on the bolster 4" from the front and rear sides of the trench, centered from side to side. Space the remaining three bars evenly in between. Coat the forms with vegetable oil or release agent, and pour the concrete.

How to Build a Brick Barbecue

1■ **After the footing has cured for one week,** use a chalk line to mark the layout for the inner edge of the fire brick wall. Make a line 4" in from the front edge of the footing, and a center line perpendicular to the first line. Make a 24 × 32" rectangle that starts at the 4" line and is centered on the center line.

2■ **Dry-lay the first course** of fire brick around the outside of the rectangle, allowing for ⅛"-thick mortar joints. Note: Proper placement of the inner walls is necessary so they can support the grills. Start with a full brick at the 4" line to start the right and left walls. Complete the course with a cut brick in the middle of the short wall.

continued next page ▶

3 ■ **Dry-lay the outer wall,** as shown here, using 4 × 3¹/₅ × 8" nominal engineer brick. Gap the bricks for ³/₈" mortar joints. The rear wall should come within ³/₈" of the last fire brick in the left inner wall. Complete the left wall with a cut brick in the middle of the wall. Mark reference lines for this outer wall.

4 ■ **Make a story pole.** On one side, mark 8 courses of fire brick, leaving a ³/₈" gap for the bottom mortar joint and ¹/₈" gaps for the remaining joints. The top of the final course should be 36" from the bottom edge. Transfer the top line to the other side of the pole. Lay out 11 courses of engineer brick, spacing them evenly so that the final course is flush with the 36" line. Each horizontal mortar joint will be slightly less than ½" thick.

5 ■ **Lay a bed** of mortar for a ³/₈" joint along the reference lines for the inner wall, then lay the first course of fire brick, using ¹/₈" joints between the bricks.

6 ■ **Lay the first course** of the outer wall, using Type N or Type S mortar. Use oiled ³/₈" dowels to create weep holes behind the front bricks of the left and right walls. Alternate laying the inner and outer walls, checking your work with the story pole and a level after every course.

7 ■ **Start the second course** of the outer wall using a half-brick butted against each side of the inner wall, then complete the course. Because there is a half-brick in the right outer wall, you need to use two three-quarter bricks in the second course to stagger the joints.

8■ **Place metal ties** between the corners of the inner and outer walls, at the second, third, fifth, and seventh courses. Use ties at the front junctions and along the rear walls. Mortar the joint where the left inner wall meets the rear outer wall.

9■ **Smooth the mortar joints** with a jointing tool when the mortar has hardened enough to resist minimal finger pressure. Check the joints in both walls after every few courses. The different mortars may need smoothing at different times.

10■ **Add tee plates for grill supports** above the fifth, sixth, and seventh courses. Use 4"-wide plates with flanges that are no more than $3/32$" thick. Position the plates along the side fire brick walls, centered 3", 12", 18", and 27" from the rear fire brick wall.

11■ **When both walls are complete,** install the capstones. Lay a bed of Type N or Type S mortar for a $3/8$"-thick joint on top of the inner and outer walls. Lay the capstone flat across the walls, keeping one end flush with the inner face of the fire brick. Make sure the bricks are level, and tool the joints when they are ready. After a week, seal the capstones and the joints between them with brick sealer and install the grills. ◆

You can cast garden borders just like these or change the mold dimensions to suit your own design. For stability, make sure the borders are at least 4" wide at the bottom.

QUIK-DATA

Cost	●	●
Skill	●	●
Time	●	●

TOOLS

Saw, drill, concrete mixing tools, rubber mallet, concrete trowel, ¾" exterior-grade plywood or melamine-covered particleboard, 2" coarse-thread drywall screws.

MATERIALS

Silicone caulk, vegetable oil or other release agent, crack-resistant concrete, plastic sheeting.

Concrete Landscape & Garden Borders

Decorative and durable edging can have any number of uses in an outdoor home. It makes great garden borders, turf edges, driveway and parking curbs, decorative tree surrounds, and barriers for loose ground covers—just to list its most popular applications. You can buy factory-made edging in masonry and other materials, but few prefab products can match the stability and longevity of poured concrete, and none can have the personal touch of a custom casting.

In this project, you'll learn how to cast your own border sections with poured concrete and a reusable wood mold. The process is so simple and the materials so inexpensive that you'll feel free to experiment with different shapes and surface treatments; see page 53 for ideas on customizing borders using trim moldings and other materials. Coloring the concrete is an even easier option for a personal decorative effect (see QUIK-TIP, below).

The best all-around concrete to use for small casting projects like this is crack-resistant concrete, which contains small fibers to add strength to the finished product without the use of metal reinforcement. However, for any casting that's less than 2" thick, use sand mix. This special concrete mix has no large aggregates, allowing it to form easily into smaller areas. Either type of concrete must cure for 48 hours before you can remove the mold; to speed your productivity, you may want to build more than one mold.

QUIK-TIP

For a personal touch, add liquid cement color to your concrete mix before pouring it into the mold. One 10 oz. bottle can color two 60-lb. or 80-lb. bags of concrete mix. Experiment with different proportions to find the right amount of color for your project.

Building a Mold for Cast Concrete

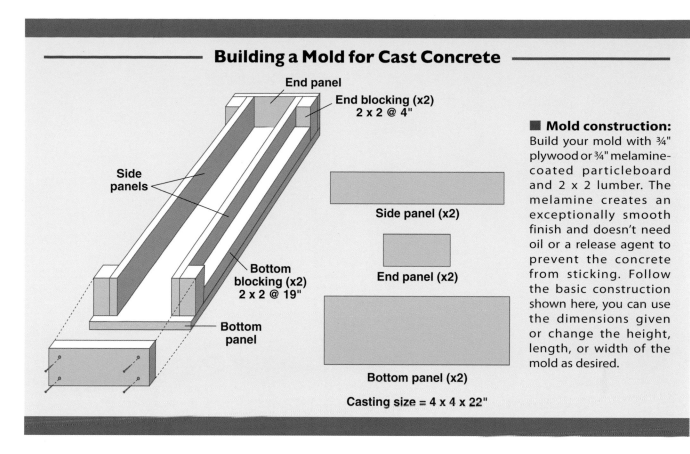

End panel

End blocking (x2)
2 x 2 @ 4"

Side panels

Bottom blocking (x2)
2 x 2 @ 19"

Bottom panel

Side panel (x2)

End panel (x2)

Bottom panel (x2)

Casting size = 4 x 4 x 22"

■ **Mold construction:**
Build your mold with ¾" plywood or ¾" melamine-coated particleboard and 2 x 2 lumber. The melamine creates an exceptionally smooth finish and doesn't need oil or a release agent to prevent the concrete from sticking. Follow the basic construction shown here, you can use the dimensions given or change the height, length, or width of the mold as desired.

How to Build Cast Concrete Borders

1■ Cut the pieces for the mold. Fasten the end blocking pieces flush with the ends of the side panels using pairs of 2" drywall screws driven through pilot holes. Fasten the bottom blocking to the side panels, flush along the bottom edges.

2■ Fasten the end panels to the end blocking with 2" screws. Install the bottom panel with screws driven through the panel and into the bottom blocking. Make sure all panels and blocking are flush along the top and bottom edges. Note: You may need to leave one end open in order to work, as we have done here.

3■ Add trim or other elements as desired for custom shaping effects (see page 53). Here, we used crown molding, which we fastened to the blocking with finish nails using a nail set. Cover the screw heads on the inside of the mold with silicone caulk; then flatten to create a smooth, flat surface.

continued next page ▶

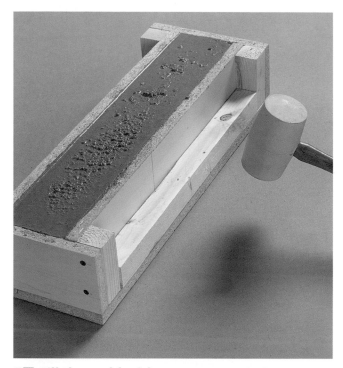

4 ■ **Coat the inside of the mold** (all nonmelamine parts) with clean vegetable oil or another release agent. Mix a batch of concrete following the product directions. An 80-lb. bag of crack-resistant concrete will fill two of the molds.

5 ■ **Fill the mold with concrete.** Settle the pour into the mold by pounding the work surface with a mallet or lifting the corners of the mold and tapping it onto the work surface.

6 ■ **Screed or trowel the concrete** so it is flat and flush with the top of the mold. Cover the mold with plastic sheeting and let it cure undisturbed for 48 hours.

7 ■ **Carefully disassemble the mold** by unscrewing the ends and bottom from the sides, as needed. Scrape, file, or grind any ragged edges for clean detailing in the finished piece. For maximum strength, set the casting in a shaded area and moist-cure it for three to five days, keeping it damp under plastic sheeting. ◆

Adding Custom Details to Border Molds

■ **To shape the top and/or side edges** of your border castings, secure pieces of wood molding or other objects into the bottom or side of the mold. The casting will come out with the relief, or negative profile, of the object.

■ **When fastening the object to the mold,** think about how you'll take the mold apart. For wood trim, fasten the pieces with finish nails, and fill the nail holes with caulk. For tile and other inlay materials, secure the tiles to the mold bottom with adhesive shelf paper; peel off the paper after removing the casting from the mold.

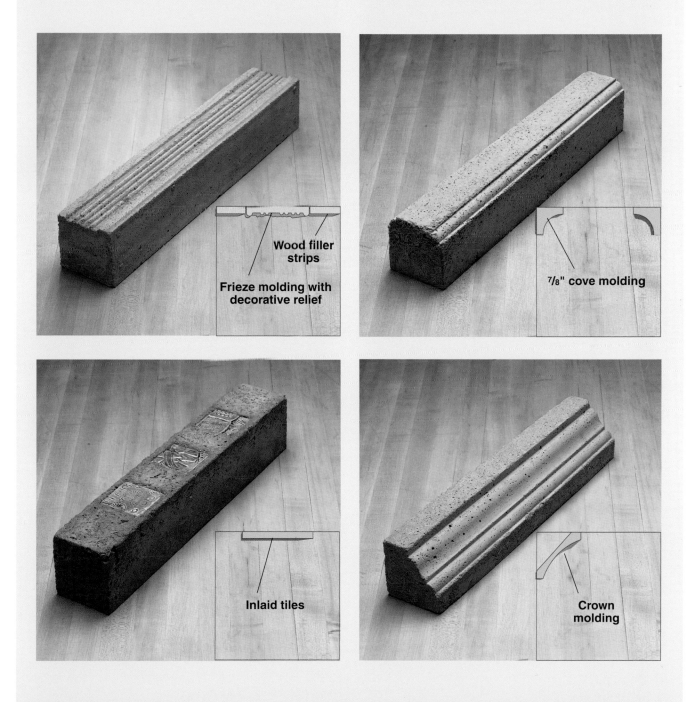

Wood filler strips

Frieze molding with decorative relief

⅞" cove molding

Inlaid tiles

Crown molding

How to Make a Poured-in-Place Border

1 ■ **Lay out the project.** Using a garden hose or rope, lay out the border design contour. The border width should be a minimum of 5".

2 ■ **Excavate the border layout** to an 8" width and 4" depth. Compact the soil to create a solid base for the concrete border.

3 ■ **Stake the contours.** Drive 1 x 1 x 12" wood stakes at 18" intervals along the contours of the curved border.

4 ■ **Attach curved forms.** Use ¼ x 4 x 8" flexible hardboard or plywood to the wood stakes using 1" wood screws.

5■ **Anchor the forms.** Cut 1 x 1" boards in lengths equal to the width of the border for use as spacers. Set 1 x 1 x 12" wood stakes along the outside contour of the border layout in 3 ft. intervals. Use 1 x 1" spacers placed along the bottom edge of the hardboard form to maintain consistent border width.

6■ **Pour the concrete.** Mix concrete to a firm workable consistency and pour into the border form. Use a margin trowel to spread and consolidate the mix.

7■ **Tool the concrete.** Once the bleed water has disappeared, smooth the surface with a wood float. Using a margin trowel, cut control joints a minimum of 1" deep into the concrete at 3-ft. intervals. Consolidate and smooth the border edges using a concrete edging tool.

8■ **Seal the concrete.** Apply acrylic concrete sealer to the concrete and let it cure for three to five days before removing the forms. Backfill against the lawn border with sod or dirt. ◆

Setting Posts in Concrete

Whether you're building a new fence or anchoring a play structure, setting the posts in concrete is the best way to make sure they'll stand straight and true for many years. Fast-setting concrete is ideal for setting posts because there's no mixing—you simply pour the dry concrete from the bag right into the hole, then add water. The concrete sets up in 20 to 40 minutes, so you can quickly move on to the next stage of the project (a great convenience when setting fence posts) or backfill the hole to finish the job. Under normal curing conditions, you can apply heavy weight to the post (a basketball backboard, for example) after just 4 hours.

The steps shown here can be used for all sorts of outdoor projects, like setting posts for mailboxes, lamps, and signs, plus flagpoles and uprights for sports and play equipment. For structural or load-bearing applications, such as concrete footings for deck posts, or for securing any post in sandy soil, follow the steps on pages 59 to 60, using concrete forms to build the footings or set the posts.

QUIK-TIP

Adding a 6" gravel base under each post and finishing the concrete base so that it slopes away from the posts are popular methods for protecting posts against rot from moisture contact.

Setting Posts in Concrete

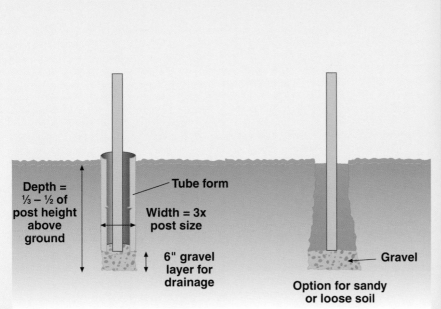

Depth = ⅓ − ½ of post height above ground

Tube form

Width = 3x post size

6" gravel layer for drainage

Gravel

Option for sandy or loose soil

1 ■ **Dig the post hole,** making it three times the width of the post and at a depth equal to ⅓ to ½ of the above-ground length of the post, plus 6" (right). For loose or sandy soil, using a tube form is recommended (left).

2 ■ **Pour 6" of gravel** or crushed stone into the bottom of the hole. Compact and level the gravel using a post or 2 x 4.

3 ■ **Set the post** in the hole. Attach angled 2 x 4 braces to two adjacent sides of the post using one screw for each brace. Drive a stake into the ground near the lower end of each brace.

4 ■ **Use a level** to position the post plumb (perfectly vertical), checking on two adjacent sides with the level, then fasten the braces to the stakes.

5 ■ **Fill the hole** with concrete up to 3 to 4" below the ground level. Add the recommended amount of water. After the concrete has set, backfill the hole with soil and/or sod.

TOOLS

Shovel, post hole digger, saw, level, concrete mixing tools, screed board or concrete trowel.

MATERIALS

Gravel or crushed stone, fast-setting concrete or concrete mix, oil or other release agent (optional), utility knife (optional), 2 x 4 bracing, QUIK-TUBE® building form.

Pouring Post Footings

When it comes to building decks and other permanent structures (particularly anything connected to your house), most building codes require foundation footings made of poured concrete. And the best way to build new footings is with concrete tube forms. Tube forms come in 6", 8", 10", and 12" diameters, in 4-ft. lengths. You can cut them to any size using a handsaw or reciprocating saw. Once the form is set in the ground, you fill it with concrete and smooth the top. The form stays in the ground, and you can trim off any above-ground portion for a finished look.

Before buying materials for your footings, consult your local building department to learn about requirements for footing size (diameter) and minimum depth. In most areas, structural footings—like house foundations—must extend below the frost line to prevent seasonal shifting during freeze-thaw cycles. Also find out how much the footings should extend above the ground (2" min. is typical) and whether you'll need to embed anchors or hardware into the wet concrete to anchor your building project.

Pouring footings in forms offers several advantages over simply filling a hole in the ground with concrete (which isn't always allowed by building codes). First, the forms are lined with wax, so water in the concrete is contained and won't leach out into the surrounding soil. This means the concrete cures slowly and evenly for maximum strength. Tube forms also help ensure footings are straight and plumb for optimum stability. And forms let you extend footings above the ground to help keep water from pooling around wood posts to prevent rot. Finally, tube forms create smooth cylinders of concrete, so they won't move with the surrounding earth as it shifts; craggy or misshapen earth-formed footings can grab the soil and move with it, defeating the purpose of building below the frost line.

Estimating Concrete for Tube Forms

Footing Depth	Number of 60-lb. Bags for Each Size (diameter of Tube)			
	6"	8"	10"	12"
1 ft.	1	1	2	2
2 ft.	1	2	3	4
3 ft.	2	3	4	6
4 ft.	2	4	5	7

Footing Depth	Number of 80-lb. Bags for Each Size (diameter of Tube)			
	6"	8"	10"	12"
1 ft.	1	1	1	2
2 ft.	1	2	2	3
3 ft.	2	3	3	4
4 ft.	2	3	4	6

How to Pour Concrete Footings

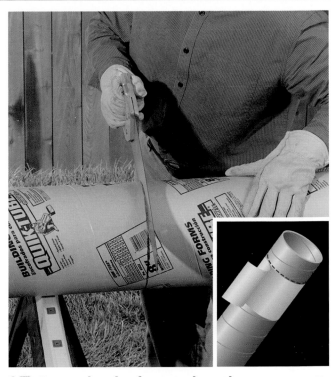

1 ▪ Dig the hole for each footing a few inches larger than the tube form diameter. The hole depth is determined by the building code; add 6" to the required depth. Fill the bottom of the hole with 6" of gravel, then tamp the gravel with a 2 x 4, wood post, or hand tamp.

2 ▪ Cut each tube form to length using a saw. To mark a straight cutting line, wrap a straightedged piece of paper around the tube. Align the edges of the paper, then mark along the paper's edge (inset). *Tip: Whenever possible, use the uncut (factory) end of the form for the top of the footing to ensure straightness.*

3 ▪ Set the tube form in the hole and hold it plumb as you backfill around it with soil. Tamp the soil firmly as you work using a shovel handle or board. Make sure the form remains plumb. *Tip: If you will strip the form later (see step 7), coat the inside with a release agent for easy removal.*

4 ▪ For footings that extend 24" or more above the ground, brace the form with wood collars, stakes, and diagonal braces. Check with a level to make sure the form is plumb before and after bracing.

continued next page ▸

5◼ Mix the concrete following the product directions. Fill the form with concrete, stabbing into the pour with a shovel to eliminate air pockets and settle the concrete. Note: Do not use a mechanical vibrator to settle the concrete. Overfill the form slightly.

6◼ Screed the top of the footing with a straight board. If desired, trowel the surface smooth, but do not overwork the concrete or trowel while bleed water is present.

▶ **Option:** Embed anchor bolts (typically a J-bolt, shown in inset) or other hardware into the wet concrete after the top is screeded flat. Make sure the hardware is plumb and positioned according to your layout; use mason's strings to check alignment of bolts.

7◼ Let the concrete cure for a day. If desired, remove the exposed portion of the form by cutting with a utility knife, then peeling the form away. Cure the footing adequately before building on it .◆

Leveling Footing

■ **When you want the tops** of your footings to be level with one another, you can mark level lines on the forms after they are set (before the concrete is placed), then fill the forms to the marked height. This is often easier than burying all of the forms so their tops are at a precise height.

■ **After securing the forms** in the ground, set up a level mason's string (using a line level) or a transit or laser level. At each form, measure down from the line and mark the form at the desired elevation in a couple of places; use the same measurement for all of the forms (photo, top). Transfer the height marks to one or two more locations around the form, then drive nails through the outside of the form at the marks (or draw a line along the inside perimeter of the form). When you place the concrete, smooth it flush with the nails to achieve the proper finished height (photo, right).

Walls &
WALL FINISHES

Concrete and masonry are timeless wall-building materials. The use of brick, stone, stucco, and concrete dates back many hundreds of years, as do countless structures built with these materials. The basic process of masonry wall building is much the same as it's always been, and constructing a low wall for your patio or landscape is a great way to take part in the time-honored traditions of bricklaying and other masonry techniques

Fortunately, what has changed over the years is the availability of premixed mortars and stucco and the development of innovative materials such as veneer stone. Like premixed bagged concrete, masonry mortars and stucco mixes are available in a full range of types each specially formulated for specific uses. One of the newest mixes is one-coat stucco, which allows you to finish a wall with a single application. And you can add color to any type of mix simply by blending the mixing water with a liquid colorant. But convenience aside, knowing that you have the right mortar, stucco, or concrete mix for your project means you can focus on the—sometimes challenging—techniques of masonry wall construction.

Veneer stone is made from lightweight concrete that's been molded and colored to look like natural stone. It costs less than real rock and is much easier to install, yet the appearance of a finished wall can be quite deceiving. Other materials you'll find in this section are concrete block, a good, economical choice for building a wall that you'll cover with stucco or tile; and poured concrete, which is just as useful for building walls as it is for flatwork and casting projects.

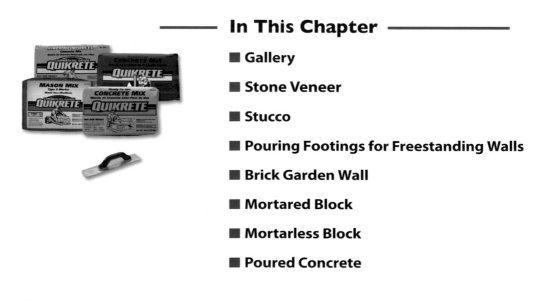

In This Chapter

- **Gallery**

- **Stone Veneer**

- **Stucco**

- **Pouring Footings for Freestanding Walls**

- **Brick Garden Wall**

- **Mortared Block**

- **Mortarless Block**

- **Poured Concrete**

GALLERY
Walls and Wall Finishes

1 ■ **Stucco** A stucco finish is an attractive, durable, low-maintenance home siding choice. Stucco can be textured and painted, so it presents a wide range of design possibilities.

2 ■ **Brick** The brick garden wall is a classic element of any formal landscape, but with a little creativity it can be an effective part of any yard or garden setting.

3 ■ **Poured concrete** A solid concrete wall shaped around a form creates a landscape portal.

4 ■ **Wall tile** can be installed over concrete or block walls that have a suitable concrete footing. Mosaic tile is a very popular choice these days.

5 ■ **Block walls** Mortared block walls create built-in seating in this patio setting.

QUIK-DATA

Cost	●	●	●	●
Skill	●	●	●	●
Time	●	●	●	●

TOOLS

Hammer or staple gun, drill, wheel-barrow, hoe, square-end trowel, circular saw, wide-mouth nippers or mason's hammer, dust mask, level, jointing tool, mortar bag, spray bottle, whisk broom.

MATERIALS

Veneer Stone, Veneer Stone Mortar or Type S mortar mix, mortar color (optional), 15# building paper, expanded galvanized metal lath (diamond mesh, minimum 2.5#), 1½" (minimum) galvanized roofing nails or heavy-duty staples, 2 × 4 lumber.

Stone Veneer

Whether you use natural or manufactured veneer, wet each stone, then apply mortar to the back before pressing it onto the mortared wall. Wetting and mortaring a stone (called buttering) results in maximum adhesion between the stone and the wall. The challenge is to arrange the stones so that large and small stones and various hues and shapes alternate across the span of the wall.

This project is designed for installing veneer stone over plywood sheathing, which has the strength to support layers of building paper. If your walls are covered with fiberboard or any other type of sheathing, ask the veneer manufacturer for recommendations.

Note: Installing from the top down makes cleanup easier since it reduces the amount of splatter on preceding courses. However, manufacturers advise bottom-up installation for some veneers. Read the manufacturer's guidelines carefully before you begin.

QUIK-TIP

Find the square footage of veneer stone required for your project by multiplying the length by the height of the area. Subtract the square footage of window and door openings and corner pieces. It's best to increase your estimate by 5 to 10 percent to allow for trimming.

Veneer Stone Mortar Calculator

Square Feet (M²)	10 (0.9)	25 (2.3)	100 (9.3)	300 (27.9)	500 (46.4)
⅜" (9.5 mm) thick - # of 80-lb (36.3 kg) bags	1	2	5	14	22
½" (12.6 mm) thick - # of 80-lb (36.3 kg) bags	1	2	6	18	30
¾" (19.1 mm) thick - # of 80-lb (36.3 kg) bags	1	3	9	27	44

All yields are approximate and do not allow for waste or uneven substrate, etc.

How to Finish Walls with Stone Veneer

1 ■ **Cover the wall with building paper,** overlapping seams by 4". Nail or staple lath every 6" into the wall studs and midway between studs. Nails or staples should penetrate 1" into the studs. Paper and lath must extend at least 16" around corners where veneer is installed.

2 ■ **Stake a level 2 × 4 against the foundation** as a temporary ledger to keep the bottom edge of the veneer 4" above grade. The gap between the bottom course and the ground will reduce staining of the veneer by plants and soil.

3 ■ **Spread out the materials** on the ground so you can select pieces of varying size, shape, and color, and create contrast in the overall appearance. Alternate the use of large and small, heavily textured and smooth, and thick and thin pieces.

4 ■ **Mix a batch of Veneer Stone Mortar** that's firm, but still workable. Mortar that's too dry or too wet is hard to work with and may fail to bond properly.

continued next page ▶

How to Finish Walls with Stone Veneer, continued

5 ■ Use a square-end trowel to press a ³/₈ to ½" layer of mortar into the lath called the scratch coat. To ensure that mortar doesn't set up too quickly, start with a 5-sq.-ft. area. Before the mortar is set use a brush or rake to roughen the surface. Allow to set hard before moving onto the next step. *Tip: Mix in small amounts of water to retemper mortar that has begun to thicken.*

6 ■ Install corner pieces first, alternating long and short legs. Dampen and apply mortar to the back of each piece, then press it firmly against the scratch coat so some mortar squeezes out. Joints between stones should be no wider than ½" and should remain as consistent as possible across the wall.

QUIK-TIP

Polymer-modified veneer stone mortar is recommended for drystack stone applications. Drystack stone is primarily bonded on one edge, requiring twice the bond strength of regular mortar.

7 ■ Set the first course of block into mortar, following the basic techniques shown on pages 154 to 155. Cut blocks as needed for the door openings. Lay the second course, offsetting the joints with the first course in a running bond pattern.

8 ■ If mortar becomes smeared on a stone, remove it with a whisk broom or soft-bristle brush after the mortar has begun to dry. Never use a wire brush or a wet brush of any kind.

9■ **Use wide-mouth nippers** or a mason's hammer to trim and shape pieces to fit. Do your best to limit trimming so each piece retains its natural look.

10■ **You can hide cut edges** that are well above or below eye level simply by rotating a stone. If an edge remains visible, use mortar to cover. Let the mortar cure for 24 hours, then remove the 2 × 4 and stakes, taking care not to dislodge any stones.

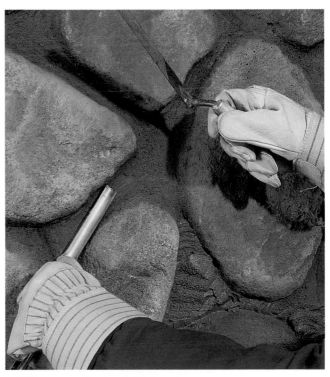

11■ **Once the wall is covered in veneer,** fill in the joints using a mortar bag and tuck-pointing mortar. Take extra care to avoid smearing the mortar. You can tint the tuck-pointing mortar to complement the veneer.

12■ **Smooth the joints** with a jointing tool once the mortar is firm. Once the mortar is dry to the touch, use a dry whisk broom to remove loose mortar—water or chemicals can leave permanent stains. ◆

Stucco is one of the most durable and low-maintenance wall finishes available, but it requires getting each stage of the installation right, as well as the mix of the stucco itself.

QUIK-DATA

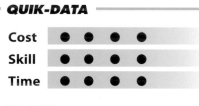

Cost	● ● ● ●
Skill	● ● ● ●
Time	● ● ● ●

TOOLS

Aviation snips, stapler, hammer, level, cement mixer, wheelbarrow, mortar hawk, square-end trowel, raking tool, darby or screed board, wood float, texturing tools, Grade D building paper, heavy-duty staples, 1½" galvanized roofing nails, self-furring galvanized metal lath (min. 2.5 lb.).

MATERIALS

Metal stucco edging, flashing, stucco mix, non-sag polyurethane sealant.

Stucco

Prized for its weather resistance, durability, and timeless beauty, stucco has long been one of the most popular exterior wall finishes. As a building material, stucco is essentially an exterior plaster made of Portland cement, sand, and water. Other ingredients may include lime, masonry cement, and various special additives for enhancing properties like crack resistance, workability, and strength. With a few exceptions, stucco is applied much as it has been for centuries—a wet mix is troweled onto the wall in successive layers, with the final coat providing the finished color and any decorative surface texture desired.

The two traditional stucco systems are the three-coat system used for standard wood-framed walls, and the two-coat system used for masonry walls, like brick, poured concrete, and concrete block. And today, there's a third process—the one-coat system—which allows you to finish standard framed walls with a single layer of stucco, saving you money and considerable time and labor over traditional three-coat applications. Each of these systems is described in detail on the opposite page.

The following pages show you an overview of the materials and basic techniques for finishing a wall with stucco. While cladding an entire house or addition is a job for professional masons, smaller projects and repair work can be much more doable for the less experienced. Fortunately, all the stucco materials you need are available in dry preblended form, so you can be sure of getting the right blend of ingredients for each application. During your planning, consult with the local building department to learn about requirements for surface preparation, fire ratings for walls, control joints, drainage, and other critical factors.

Base Coat Stucco Calculator

Square Feet (M²)	10 (0.9)	25 (2.3)	100 (9.3)	300 (27.9)	500 (46.4)
⅜" (9.5 mm) thick - # of 80-lb (36.3 kg) bags	1	1	4	12	19
½" (12.6 mm) thick - # of 80-lb (36.3 kg) bags	1	2	6	16	26
¾" (18.8 mm) thick - # of 80-lb (36.3 kg) bags	1	2	8	24	38

All yields are approximate and do not allow for waste or uneven substrate, etc.

Stucco Systems

■ **Three-coat stucco** is the traditional application for stud-framed walls covered with plywood, oriented strand board (OSB), or rigid foam insulation sheathing. It starts with two layers of Grade D building paper for a moisture barrier. The wall is then covered with self-furring, expanded metal lath fastened to the framing with galvanized nails.

■ **The scratch coat** is the first layer of stucco. It is pressed into the lath then smoothed to a flat layer about ³⁄₈" thick. While still wet, the stucco is "scratched" with a raking tool to create horizontal keys for the next layer to adhere to.

■ **The brown coat** is the next layer. It's about ³⁄₈"-thick and brings the wall surface to within ¹⁄₈" to ¹⁄₄" of the finished thickness. Imperfections here can easily telegraph through the thin final coat, so the surface must be smooth and flat. To provide tooth for the final layer, the brown coat is finished with a wood float for a slightly roughened texture.

■ **The finish coat** completes the treatment, bringing the surface flush with the stucco trim pieces and providing the color and decorative texture, if desired. There are many options for texturing stucco; a few of the classic ones are shown on page 75.

■ **Two-coat stucco** is the standard treatment for masonry walls. This system is the same as a three-coat treatment but without a scratch coat. The base coat on a two-coat system is the same as the brown coat on a three-coat system. For the base coat to bond well, the masonry surface must be clean, unpainted, and sufficiently porous. You can test this by spraying water onto the surface: if the water beads and runs down the wall, apply bonding adhesive before applying the base coat, or you can fasten self-furring metal lath directly to the wall, then apply a full three-coat stucco treatment.

■ **One-coat stucco** is a single-layer system for finishing framed walls prepared with a waterproof barrier and metal lath (as with a three-coat system). This treatment calls for one-coat, fiberglass-reinforced stucco, a special formulation that contains ½" alkali-resistant fiberglass fiber and other additives to combine high-performance characteristics with greatly simplified application. This stucco is applied in a ³⁄₈- to ⁵⁄₈"-thick layer using standard techniques. QUIKRETE One Coat Fiberglass Reinforced Stucco meets code requirements for a one-hour firewall over wood and form systems.

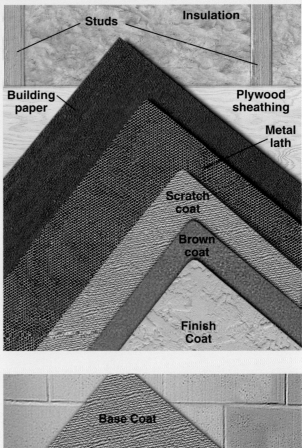

Studs
Insulation
Building paper
Plywood sheathing
Metal lath
Scratch coat
Brown coat
Finish Coat

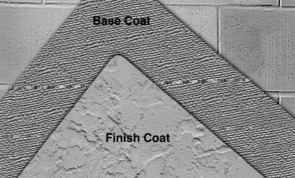

Base Coat
Finish Coat

continued next page ▶

Premixed Stucco Products

■ **Finding the right blend of ingredients** and mixing to the proper consistency are critical to the success of any stucco project. Premixed stucco eliminates the guesswork by giving you the perfect blend in each bag, along with mixing and curing instructions for a professional-quality job. All of the stucco products shown here are sold in complete form, meaning all you do is add water before application. Be sure to follow the mixing and curing instructions carefully for each product.

■ **Scratch and Brown, Base Coat Stucco:** Use this premixed stucco for both the scratch and brown coats of a three-coat application or for the base coat of a two-coat system. You can apply the mixed stucco with a trowel or an approved sprayer. Available in 80-lb. bags in gray color. Each bag yields approximately 0.83 cu. ft. or an applied coverage of approximately 27 sq. ft. at ⅜" thickness.

■ **Finish Coat Stucco:** Use this stucco for the finish coat on both three-coat and two-coat systems. You can also use it to create a decorative textured finish over one-coat stucco. Apply Finish Coat stucco to a minimum thickness of ⅛", then texture the surface as desired. Available in gray and white for achieving a full range of colors (see below). Coverage of 80-lb. bag is approximately 70 sq. ft. at ⅛" thickness.

■ **One-Coat, Fiberglass-Reinforced Stucco:** Complete your stucco application in one step with this convenient all-in-one stucco mix. You can texture the surface of the single layer or add a top coat of Finish Coat stucco for special decorative effects. Available in 80-lb. bags. An 80-lb. bag covers approximately 25 sq. ft. of wall at ⅜" thickness.

■ **Stucco and Mortar Color:** Available in 20 standard colors, Stucco & Mortar Color is a permanent liquid colorant that you blend with the stucco mix before application. Some colors are for use with gray stucco mix, while many others are compatible with white mix. For best results, combine the liquid colorant with the mixing water before adding the dry stucco mix, then blend thoroughly until the color is uniform.

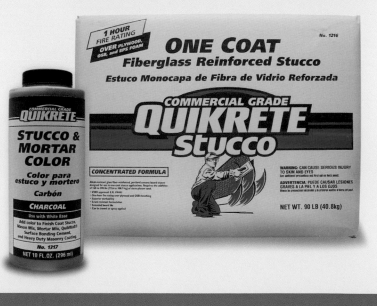

Preparing Framed Walls for Stucco

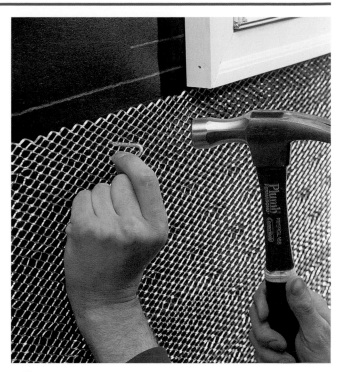

1■ **Attach building paper** over exterior wall sheathing using heavy-duty staples or roofing nails. Overlap sheets by 4". Usually, two layers of paper are required or recommended; consult your local building department for code requirements in your area.

2■ **Install self-furring expanded metal lath** over the building paper with staples or 1½" galvanized roofing nails (don't use aluminum nails) driven into the wall studs every 6". Overlap sheets of lath by 1" on horizontal seams and 2" on vertical seams. Install the lath with the rougher side facing out.

3■ **Install metal edging** for clean, finished lines at vertical edges of walls. Install casing bead along the top of stuccoed areas and weep screed (or drip screed) along the bottom edges, as applicable. Make sure all edging is level and plumb, and fasten it with galvanized roofing nails. Add flashing as needed over windows and doors.

4■ **Use aviation snips** to trim sheets of lath or cut edging materials to length. Cut lath and edging can be very sharp, so always wear gloves when working with these materials. ◆

How to Finish Walls with Stucco

1■ **For a three-coat system,** mix the stucco to a trowel-able consistency and apply it with a square trowel, working from the bottom up. Press the stucco into the lath, then screed and smooth the surface for a uniform thickness. When the coat hardens enough to hold a finger impression, scratch ⅛"-deep horizontal grooves into the surface with a raking tool.

2■ **After moist-curing the scratch coat** for 24 to 48 hours, mix stucco for the brown coat (or base coat for two-coat system) and apply it in a ⅜"-thick layer. Use a straight board or a darby to screed the surface so it's flat and even. When the stucco has lost its sheen, float it with a wood trowel to roughen the surface. Moist-cure the coat for 48 hours as directed.

▶**Variation:** For a one-coat application, mix a fiber reinforced one-coat stucco and apply it in a ⅜ to ⅝"-thick layer, working from the bottom up and forcing it in to completely embed the lath. Screed the surface flat with a darby or board. When the surface loses its sheen, finish trowel or texture the surface as desired. Cure the coat as directed. Seal all joints around building elements with polyurethane sealant.

3■ **Mix the finish coat** and apply it in a ⅛"-thick (minimum) layer, working from the bottom up. Complete large sections or entire walls at one time for color consistency. Texture the surface as desired. Cure the coat as directed. Seal all joints around building elements with polyurethane sealant. ◆

Finishing Stucco

1■ **Test the coloring** of finish stucco by adding different proportions of colorant and mix. Let the samples dry to see their true finished color. For the application batches, be sure to use the same proportions when mixing each batch.

2■ **Mix the finish batch** so it contains slightly more water than the scratch and brown coats. The mix should still stay on the mortar hawk without running.

▶**Finish Option:** Cover a float with carpet to make an ideal tool for achieving a float-finish texture. Experiment on a small area.

▶**Finish Option:** Achieve a wet-dash finish by flinging, or dashing, stucco onto the surface. Let the stucco cure undisturbed.

▶**Finish Option:** For a dash-trowel texture, dash the surface with stucco using a whisk broom (left), then flatten the stucco by troweling over it. ◆

Poured Footings for Freestanding Walls

QUIK-DATA

Cost	●	●	
Skill	●	●	
Time	●	●	●

TOOLS

Rope, carpenter's square, hand maul, tape measure, mason's string, line level, spade, sod cutter, straightedge, level, wheelbarrow, shovel, hand tamper, circular saw, reciprocating saw, float, drill.

MATERIALS

Concrete mix, water, #3 rebar, 16-gauge wire, 2 × 4 lumber, 3" screws, compactible gravel, vegetable oil or commercial release agent.

Footings provide a stable, level base for brick, block, stone, and poured concrete structures. They distribute the weight of the structure evenly, prevent sinking, and keep structures from moving during seasonal freeze-thaw cycles.

The required depth of a footing is usually determined by the frost line, which varies by region. The frost line is the point nearest ground level where the soil does not freeze. In colder climates, it is likely to be 48" or deeper. Frost footings (footings designed to keep structures from moving during freezing temperatures) should extend a minimum of 6 to 12" below the frost line for the area.

Footings are required for concrete, stone, brick, and block structures that adjoin other permanent structures or that exceed the height specified by local codes. Frost footings extend 6 to 12" below the frost line. Slab footings, which are typically 8" thick, may be recommended for low, freestanding structures built using mortar or poured concrete. Before starting your project, ask a building inspector about footing recommendations and requirements for your area.

QUIK-TIP

To speed up your project, use QUIKRETE® fast-setting concrete mix for your footing. You can build on the footing in just 24 hours versus seven days for standard concrete.

▶Options for Forming Footings

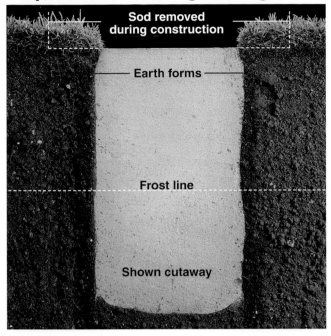

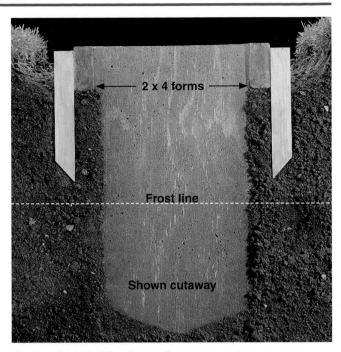

■ **For poured concrete,** use the earth as a form. Strip sod from around the project area, then strike off the concrete with a screed board resting on the earth at the edges of the top of the trench.

■ **For brick, block, and stone,** build level, recessed wood forms. Rest the screed board on the frames when you strike off the concrete to create a flat, even surface for stacking masonry units.

Tips for Building Footings

■ **Make footings twice as wide** as the wall or structure they will support. They also should extend at least 12" past the ends of the project area.

■ **Add tie-rods** if you will be pouring concrete over the footing. Before the concrete hardens, press 12" sections of rebar 6" into the concrete. The tie-rods will anchor the footing to the structure it supports.

How to Pour a Footing

1■ Make a rough outline of the footing using a rope or hose. Outline the project area with stakes and mason's string.

2■ Strip away sod 6" outside the project area on all sides, then excavate the trench for the footing to a depth 12" below the frost line.

3■ Build and install a 2 × 4 form frame for the footing, aligning it with the mason's strings. Stake the form in place, and adjust to level.

▶Variation: If your project abuts another structure, such as a house foundation, slip a piece of asphalt-impregnated fiber board into the trench to create an isolation joint between the footing and the structure. Use a few dabs of construction adhesive to hold it in place.

4 ■ **Make two #3 rebar grids** to reinforce the footing. For each grid, cut two pieces of #3 rebar 8" shorter than the length of the footing, and two pieces 4" shorter than the depth of the footing. Bind the pieces together with 16-gauge wire, forming a rectangle. Set the rebar grids upright in the trench, leaving 4" of space between the grids and the walls of the trench. Coat the inside edge of the form with vegetable oil or commercial release agent.

5 ■ Mix and pour concrete so it reaches the tops of the forms. Screed the surface using a 2 × 4. Float the concrete until it is smooth and level.

6 ■ **Cure the concrete for one week** before you build on the footing. Remove the forms and backfill around the edges of the footing. ◆

Buttering is a term used to describe the process of applying mortar to the end of a brick or block before adding it to the structure being built. Apply a heavy layer of mortar to one end of a brick, then cut off the excess with a trowel.

Cost ● ● ●
Skill ● ● ● ●
Time ● ● ● ●

TOOLS

Gloves, trowel, chalk line, level, line blocks, mason's string, jointing tool.

MATERIALS

Mortar (Type S or N), brick, wall ties, rebar (optional).

Brick Garden Wall

Patience, care, and good technique are the key elements to building brick structures that have a professional look. Start with a sturdy, level footing (pages 76 to 79), and don't worry if your initial bricklaying attempts aren't perfect. Survey your work often and stop when you spot a problem. As long as the mortar's still soft, you can remove bricks and try again.

This section features one method of brick wall construction: laying up the ends of the wall first, then filling in the interior bricks. The alternate method, laying one course at a time, is shown with concrete block (pages 84 to 87).

Mason Mix Calculator

Number of bags required to lay bricks ³/₈" joint (9mm)

Number of Bricks (Standard)	30	50	75	100	180	250	400	800	1500
80-lb Bags (36.3 kg)	1	2	3	3	5	7	11	22	41

How to Build a Double-wythe Brick Wall

1 **Dry-lay the first course** by setting down two parallel rows of brick spaced ¾ to 1" apart. Use a chalk line to outline the location of the wall on the slab. Draw pencil lines on the slab to mark the end of each brick. Test-fit the spacing with a ⅜"-diameter dowel, then mark the locations of the joint gaps to use as a reference after the spacers are removed.

2 **Dampen the concrete slab** or footing with water, and dampen the bricks or blocks if necessary. Mix mortar and place a layer of mortar onto the footing for the first two bricks of one wythe at one end of the layout. Butter the inside end of the first brick, then press the brick into the mortar, creating a ⅜" mortar bed. Cut away excess mortar.

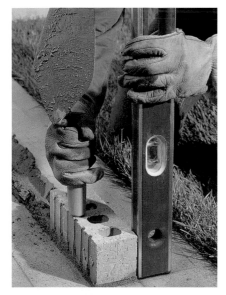

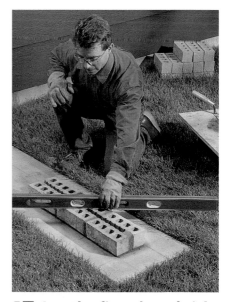

3 **Plumb the face** of the end brick using a level. Tap lightly with the handle of the trowel to correct the brick if it is not plumb. Level the brick end to end. Butter the end of a second brick, then set it into the mortar bed, pushing the dry end toward the first brick to create a joint of ⅜".

4 **Butter and place** a third brick using the chalk lines as a general reference, then using a level to check for level and plumb. Adjust any bricks that are not aligned by tapping lightly with the trowel handle.

5 **Lay the first three bricks** for the other wythe parallel to the first wythe. Level the wythes, and make sure the end bricks and mortar joints align. Fill the gaps between the wythes at each end with mortar.

continued next page ▶

6■ Cut a half brick, then throw and furrow a mortar bed for a half brick on top of the first course. Butter the end of the half brick, then set the half brick in the mortar bed, creating a ³/₈" joint. Cut away excess mortar. Make sure bricks are plumb and level.

7■ Add more bricks and half bricks to both wythes at the end until you lay the first bricks in the fourth course. Align bricks with the reference lines. Note: To build corners, lay a header brick at the end of two parallel wythes. Position the header brick in each subsequent course perpendicular to the header brick in the previous course (inset).

8■■ Check the spacing of the end bricks with a straightedge. Properly spaced bricks form a straight line when you place the straightedge over the stepped end bricks. If bricks are not in alignment, do not move those bricks already set. Try to compensate for the problem gradually as you fill in the middle (field) bricks (step 9) by slightly reducing or increasing the spacing between joints.

9■■ Every 30 minutes, stop laying bricks and prepare to smooth out all the untooled mortar joints with a jointing tool. Mortar joints should be smoothed (struck) when mortar is thumbprint hard. Do the horizontal joints first, then the vertical joints. Cut away any excess mortar pressed from the joints using a trowel. When the mortar has set but is not too hard, brush any excess mortar from the brick faces.

Line block

10■ Build the opposite end of the wall with the same methods as the first using the chalk lines as a reference. Stretch a mason's string between the two ends to establish a flush, level line between ends—use line blocks to secure the string. Pull the string until it is taut. Begin to fill in the field bricks (the bricks between ends) on the first course using the mason's string as a guide.

11 ■ **Lay the remaining field bricks.** The last brick, called the closure brick, should be buttered at both ends. Center the closure brick between the two adjoining bricks, then set in place with the trowel handle. Fill in the first three courses of each wythe, moving the mason's string up one course after completing each course.

Metal wall tie

12 ■ **In the fourth course,** embed metal wall ties into the mortar bed of one wythe and on top of the brick adjacent to it. Space the ties 2 to 3 ft. apart, every three courses. For added strength, set metal rebar into the cavities between the wythes and fill with thin mortar.

13 ■ **Lay the remaining courses,** installing metal ties every third course. Check with mason's string frequently for alignment, and use a level to make sure the wall is plumb and level.

14 ■ **Lay a furrowed mortar bed** on the top course, and place a wall cap on top of the wall to cover empty spaces and provide a finished appearance. Remove any excess mortar. Make sure the cap blocks are aligned and level. Fill the joints between cap blocks with mortar. ◆

Mortared Block

Block walls can be built fairly quickly because of the size of the individual blocks. Still, the same patience and attention to detail involved in laying blocks are required. Check your work often, and don't be afraid to back up a step or two to correct your mistakes.

This section features a concrete block wall laid up one course at a time. Make sure you have a sturdy, level footing (page 76 to 79) before you start.

QUIK-DATA

Cost	●	●	●	
Skill	●	●	●	●
Time	●	●	●	●	●

TOOLS
Trowel, chalk line, level, mason's string, line blocks, jointing tool.

MATERIALS
Mortar mix (Type S or N), 8 × 8" concrete blocks, stakes, cap blocks, rebar, wire reinforcing strips.

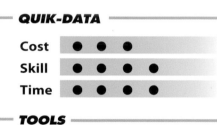
QUIK-TIP

Dampen the block before placing mortar for improved bond strength.

How to Lay Concrete Block

1 ▪ Dry-lay the first course, leaving a ³/₈" gap between blocks. Draw reference lines on the concrete base to mark the ends of the row, extending the lines well past the edges of the block. Use a chalk line to snap reference lines on each side of the base 3" from the blocks. These reference lines will serve as a guide when setting the blocks into mortar.

2 ▪ Dampen the concrete slab or footing with water, and dampen the blocks if necessary. Mix mortar and place a layer of mortar on to the footing for the first two blocks at one end of the layout. Butter the inside end of the first block, then press the block into the mortar, creating a ³/₈" mortar bed. The mortar should be firm enough to support the weight of the first block course.

Mason Mix Calculator

Number of bags required to lay blocks ³/₈" joint (9mm)

Number of Blocks (8 x 8 x 16")	10	15	25	30	50	100	125	500	1000
80-lb Bags (36.3 kg)	1	2	3	3	5	9	11	42	84

3■ **Set a combination** corner block into the mortar bed. Press it into the mortar to create a ³/₈"-thick bed joint. Hold the block in place and cut away the excess mortar (save excess mortar for the next section of the mortar bed). Check the block with a level to make sure it is level and plumb. Make any necessary adjustments by rapping on the high side with the handle of a trowel. Be careful not to displace too much mortar.

4■ **Drive a stake** at each end of the project and attach one end of a mason's string to each stake. Thread a line level onto the string and adjust the string until it is level and flush with the top of the corner block. Place a mortar bed and set a corner block at the other end. Adjust the block so it is plumb and level, making sure it is aligned with the mason's string.

5■ **Place a mortar bed** for the second block at one end of the project: butter one end of a standard block and set it next to the corner block, pressing the two blocks together so the joint between them is ³/₈" thick. Tap the block with the handle of a trowel to set it, and adjust the block until it is even with the mason's string. Be careful to maintain the ³/₈" joint.

6■ **Install all but the last block** in the first course, working from the ends toward the middle. Align the blocks with the mason's string. Clean excess mortar from the base before it hardens.

continued next page ▶

7■ **Butter the flanges** on both ends of a standard block for use as the closure block in the course. Slide the closure block into the gap between blocks, keeping the mortar joints an even thickness on each side. Align the block with the mason's string.

8■ **Apply a 1"-thick mortar bed** for the half block at one end of the wall, then begin the second course with a half block.

QUIK-TIP

Buttering a concrete block involves laying narrow slices of mortar on the two flanges at the end of the block. It is not necessary to butter the valley between the flanges unless the project calls for it.

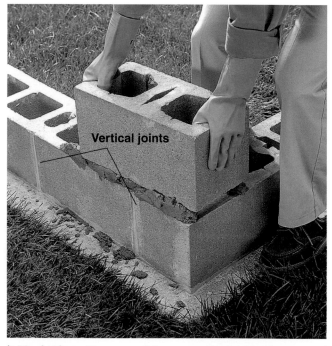

Vertical joints

9■ **Set the half block** into the mortar bed with the smooth surfaces facing out. Use the level to make sure the half block is plumb with the first corner block, then check to make sure it is level. Adjust as needed. Install a half block at the other end.

▶**Variation:** If your wall has a corner, begin the second course with a full-sized end block that spans the vertical joint formed where the two walls meet. This layout creates and maintains a running bond pattern for the wall.

10■ **Attach a mason's string** for reference, securing it either with line blocks or a nail. If you do not have line blocks, insert a nail into the wet mortar at each end of the wall, then wind the mason's string around and up to the top corner of the second course, as shown above. Connect both ends and draw the mason's string taut. Place a mortar bed for the next block, then fill out the second course using the mason's string as a reference line.

11■ **Smooth (strike)** the fresh mortar joints with a jointing tool when mortar is thumbprint hard, and remove any excess mortar. Tool the horizontal joints first, then the vertical joints. Cut off excess mortar using a trowel blade. When the mortar has set but is not too hard, brush any excess mortar from the block faces. Continue building the wall until it is complete.

■ **Option: When building stack bond walls** with vertical joints that are in alignment, use wire reinforcing strips in the mortar beds every third course (or as required by local codes) to increase the strength of the wall. The wire should be completely embedded in the mortar.

12■ **Install a wall cap** on top of the wall to cover the empty spaces and create a finished appearance. Set the cap pieces into mortar beds, then butter an end with mortar. Level the cap, then tool to match the joints in the rest of the wall. ◆

Surface bonding cement gives a dry-stacked block wall an attractive finished appearance. It also binds the blocks together. Lightly dampen the blocks (inset) before applying the product.

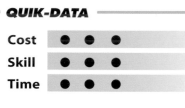

Mortarless Block

The project shown here demonstrates how to lay a mortarless concrete block wall that is coated with surface-bonding cement. Surface-bonding cement contains thousands of fiberglass fibers that interlock when the product cures, giving the wall greater flexural strength than an ordinary mortared block wall. The finished appearance of walls coated with surface-bonding cement resembles stucco. It is ideal for garden walls, stucco fence walls, trash can enclosures, mobile home skirting, and as a waterproof coating for concrete ponds when used with acrylic fortifier.

QUIK-DATA

Cost	●	●	●
Skill	●	●	●
Time	●	●	●

TOOLS

Aviation snips, mason's trowel, brickset, chisel, maul, mason's string, level, chalk line, line blocks.

MATERIALS

Concrete block, metal ties, wire mesh, Quikwall surface-bonding cement, stucco and mortar color (optional).

QUIK-TIP

For extra strength, fill every other block cavity with concrete.

How to Lay a Mortarless Block Wall

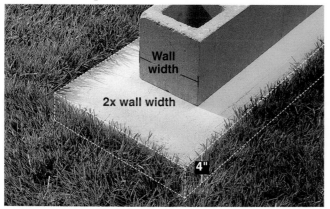

Wall width

2x wall width

4"

1 ■ **Start with a dry layout** of the first course on a concrete footing. Where less than half a block is needed, trim two blocks instead. For example, where three and one-third block lengths are required, use four blocks, and cut two of them to two-thirds their length. You'll end up with a stronger, more durable wall.

2 ■ **Mark the corners** of the end blocks on the footing with a pencil. Then, remove the blocks and snap chalk lines to indicate where to lay the mortar bed and the initial course of block.

3 ■ **Mist the footing with water**, then lay a ¾" thick bed of mortar on the footing. Take care to cover only the area inside the reference lines. The mortar must be firm enough to prevent the first course from sagging.

4 ■ **Lay the first course,** starting at one end and placing blocks in the mortar bed with no spacing in between. Use solid-faced blocks on the ends of the wall and check the course for level. If your wall is longer than 20 ft., consider inclusion of an expansion joint.

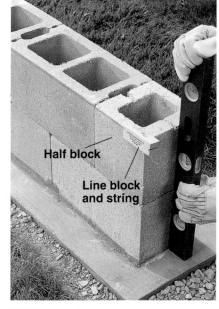

Half block

Line block and string

5 ■ **Lay subsequent courses** one at a time using a level to check for plumb and line blocks to check for level. Begin courses with solid-faced blocks at each end. Use half blocks, to establish a running bond pattern. For walls over 6 ft. tall, consult local building codes.

6 ■ **Mix the surface bonding cement** thoroughly in a mortar box until it achieves a firm, workable consistency. Eliminate all lumps during mixing. If you are coloring the surface bonding cement, add the coloring agent directly to the mixing water prior to mixing the product.

7 ■ **Apply surface bonding cement** in a ¼"-thick layer. Work from the bottom of the wall to the top. A variety of stucco textures can be added to the wall as soon as it becomes thumbprint hard. ◆

In any setting, a poured concrete wall offers clean, sleek lines and a reassuringly solid presence. You can leave the wall exposed to display its natural coloring and texture. For a custom design element, you can add color to the concrete mix or decorate any of the wall's surfaces with stucco, tile, or other masonry finishes.

QUIK-DATA

Cost	● ● ●
Skill	● ● ● ●
Time	● ● ● ●

TOOLS

Drill and ¹/₈" bit; hacksaw or recip-rocating saw; pliers; level; concrete mixing tools; shovel; concrete trowel; 2 x 4, 2 x 2, and 1 x 2 lumber; 16d and 8d nails; 3/4" exterior-grade plywood; #3 steel reinforcing bar (rebar); 8-gauge tie wire; wood screws or deck screws; vegetable oil or commercial release agent.

MATERIALS

Concrete mix or QUIKRETE® 5000; plastic sheeting; quick-setting cement (mixed with concrete acrylic fortifier) or fast-set repair mortar, exterior-use anchoring cement, heavy-duty masonry coating (optional).

Poured Concrete Wall

Building vertically with poured concrete introduces a whole new dimension to this ever-versatile material. And as much as walls may seem more challenging than slabs or casting projects, the basic building process is just as simple and straightforward. You construct forms using ordinary materials, then fill them with concrete and finish the surface. While tall concrete walls and load-bearing structures require careful engineering and professional skills, a low partition wall for a patio or garden can be a great do-it-yourself project.

The first rule of concrete wall building is knowing that the entire job relies on the strength of the form. A cubic foot of concrete weighs about 140 pounds, which means that a 3-foot-tall wall that is 6 inches thick weighs 210 pounds. for each linear foot. If the wall is 10 feet long, the form must contain over a ton of wet concrete. And the taller the wall, the greater the pressure on the base of the form. If the form has a weak spot and the concrete breaks through (known in the trades as a blowout), there's little chance of saving the project. So be sure to brace, stake, and tie your form carefully.

This project shows you the basic steps for building a 3-foot-high partition wall. This type of wall can typically be built on a poured concrete footing or a reinforced slab that's at least 4 inches thick. When planning your project, consult your local building department for specific requirements such as wall size, footing specifications, and metal reinforcement in the wall. Note: This wall design is not suitable for retaining walls, tall walls, or load-bearing walls.

For help with building a new footing, see pages 76 to 79. The footing should be at least 12" wide (2x wall thickness) and at least 6" thick (1x wall thickness), and it must extend below the frost line (or in accordance with the local building code). If your wall will stand on a concrete patio or other slab, the sidebar on page 93 shows you how to install rebar in the slab for anchoring the wall.

Wall Form Construction

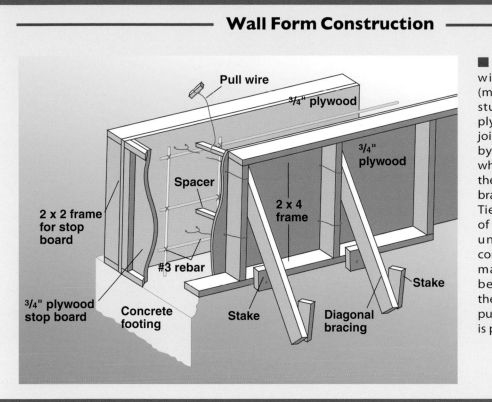

Pull wire

¾" plywood

¾" plywood

Spacer

2 x 4 frame

2 x 2 frame for stop board

#3 rebar

Stake

¾" plywood stop board

Concrete footing

Stake

Diagonal bracing

■ **A wall form** is built with two framed sides (much like a standard 2 x 4 stud wall) covered with ¾" plywood. The two sides are joined together at each end by means of a stop board, which also shapes the end of the finished wall. The form is braced and staked in position. Tie wires prevent the sides of the form from spreading under the force of the concrete. Temporary spacers maintain proper spacing between the sides while the form is empty; these are pulled out once the concrete is placed.

How to Create a Poured Concrete Wall

1■ **Build the frames for the form sides** from 2 x 4 lumber and 16d nails. Include a stud at each end and every 16" in between. Plan an extra 2¼" of wall length for each stop board. For walls longer than 8 ft., build additional frames.

2■ **Cut one piece of ¾" plywood** for each side frame. Fasten the plywood to frames with 8d nails driven through the plywood and into the framing. Make sure the top edges of the panels are straight and flush with the frames.

continued next page ▶

3 ■ **Drill holes for the tie wires:** At each stud location, drill two pairs of ⅛" holes evenly spaced, and keep the holes close to the stud faces. Drill matching holes on the other form side.

4 ■ **Cut #3 rebar at 34",** one piece for each rebar anchor in the footing. Cut rebar for three horizontal runs, 4" shorter than the wall length. Tie the short pieces to the footing anchors using 8-gauge tie wire, then tie the horizontal pieces to the verticals, spacing them 12" apart and keeping their ends 2" from the wall ends. To make a 90° turn, bend the bars on one leg of the wall so they overlap the others by 24".

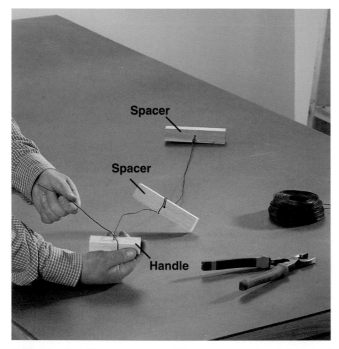

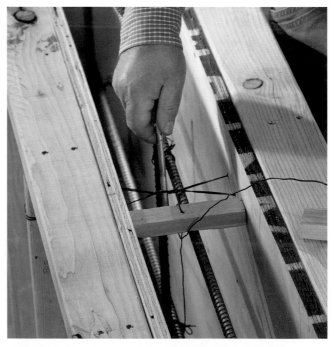

5 ■ **Cut 1 x 2 spacers at 6",** one piece for each set of tie wire holes. These temporary spacers will be used to maintain the form width. Tie each pair of spacers to a pull wire, spacing them to match the hole spacing. Then attach a piece of scrap wood to the end of the pull wire to serve as a handle.

6 ■ **Set the form sides in place.** Install the stop boards with 2 x 2 frames for backing; fasten the frames to the form sides with screws. Tie a loop of wire through each set of tie wire holes, and position a spacer near each loop. Use a stick to twist the loop strands together, pulling the form sides inward, tight against the spacers.

Building on a Concrete Slab

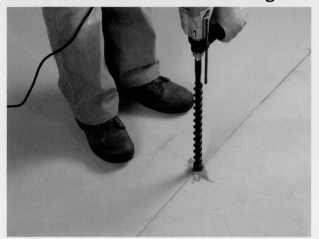

■ **A standard, reinforced** 4"-thick concrete slab can be a suitable foundation for a low partition wall like the one shown in this project. The slab must be in good condition, with no significant cracks or changes in level, and you should place the wall several inches away from the slab edge to ensure adequate support.

To anchor the new wall to the slab and provide lateral stability, you'll need to install rebar anchors in the slab, following the basic steps shown here. But before going ahead with the project, be sure to have your plans approved by the local building department.

■ **Mark the locations** for the rebar anchors along the wall center: position an anchor 4" from each end of the wall and every 24" in between. At each location, drill a 1½"-diameter hole straight down into the concrete using a hammer drill and 1½" masonry bit (above, left). Make the holes 3" deep. Spray out the holes to remove all dust and debris using an air compressor with a trigger-type nozzle. Cut six pieces of #4 rebar at 16". Mix exterior-use anchoring cement to a pourable consistency. Insert the rods into the holes, then fill the hole with the cement (above, right). Hold the rods plumb until the cement sets (about 10 minutes). Let the cement cure for 24 hours.

Securing Braces on a Concrete Slab

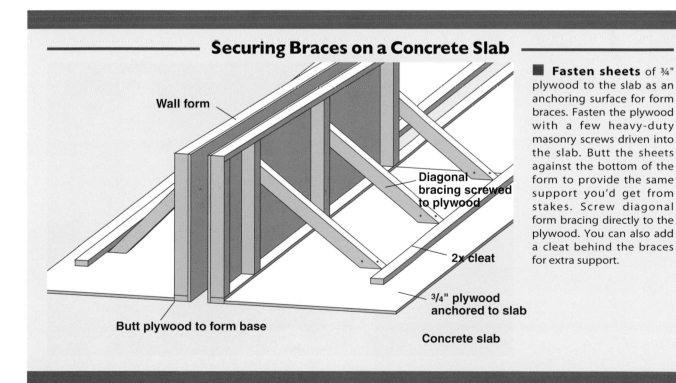

Wall form

Diagonal bracing screwed to plywood

2x cleat

3/4" plywood anchored to slab

Butt plywood to form base

Concrete slab

■ **Fasten sheets** of ¾" plywood to the slab as an anchoring surface for form braces. Fasten the plywood with a few heavy-duty masonry screws driven into the slab. Butt the sheets against the bottom of the form to provide the same support you'd get from stakes. Screw diagonal form bracing directly to the plywood. You can also add a cleat behind the braces for extra support.

continued next page ▶

7 ■ Make sure the form is centered over the footing. Check that the sides are plumb and the top is level. Secure the form with stakes and braces: install a diagonal brace at each stud location, and stake along the bottom of the form sides every 12". Fasten all stakes and braces to the form framing with screws. For long walls, join additional side pieces with screws for a tight joint with no gapping along the plywood seam. Brace the studs directly behind the joint point between sections. Coat the insides of the form with a release agent. If building on a slab (above, right), construct the form and then attach as a unit (see page 93).

8 ■ Mix the first batches of concrete in a power mixer, being careful not to add too much water—a soupy mix results in weakened concrete.

9 ■ Place the concrete in the forms. Start at the ends and work toward the center, filling the form about halfway up (no more than 20" deep). Rap on the forms to settle out air bubbles and then fill to the top. Remove the spacers as you proceed.

10 ■ **Use a shovel to stab** into the concrete to work it around the rebar and eliminate air pockets. Continue to rap the sides of the forms with a hammer or mallet to help settle the concrete against the forms.

11 ■ **Screed the top of the wall** flat with a 2 x 4, removing spacers as you work. After the bleed water disappears, float or trowel the top surface of the wall for the desired finish. Also round over the edges of the wall with an edger, if desired.

12 ■ **Cover the wall with plastic** and let it cure for two or three days. Remove the plastic. Sprinkle with water on hot or dry days to keep concrete from drying too quickly.

13 ■ **Cut the loops of tie wire** and remove the forms. Trim the tie wires below the surface of the concrete, and then patch the depressions with quick-setting cement or fast-set repair mortar. Trowel the patches flush with the wall surface. ◆

QUIK-TIP

To achieve a consistent wall color and texture apply heavy duty masonry coating with acrylic fortifier using a masonry brush.

Indoor
PROJECTS

Today, some of the best concrete projects are accomplished indoors. The growth in popularity of concrete countertops is largely responsible for the renewal of interest in interior concrete and masonry projects. In fact, the applications for concrete countertop techniques have expanded to include bathroom vanities and even fireplace hearths. But the possibilities for beautifying the inside of your home with concrete and masonry go well beyond slab-type structures.

Glass block may not be the first product that leaps to mind when you think of masonry, but it is very much a masonry product that is installed in much the same way as brick. As the number of styles and sizes of glass block grows, creative designers are constantly finding new uses for the versatile material throughout the home. In this chapter we reveal how to use glass block for one of its most popular items: a glass block shower wall.

Concrete floors aren't just for basements anymore. Increasingly, modern designers and architects are including the beauty of concrete floors into practically any room in the house. One reason for this is the availability of new acid etching products that produce stained concrete floors with rich colors and textures. Equally popular outdoors on patio areas, staining concrete is an easy way to create an upscale look in an instant.

— In This Chapter —

■ **Kitchen Countertop**

■ **Glass Block Shower**

■ **Acid-Stained Concrete Floor**

Building a custom concrete countertop like this is an easier project than you might think. All of the building materials and techniques are covered in this book.

QUIK-DATA

Cost	●	●	●	●
Skill	●	●	●	●	●
Time	●	●	●	●	●

TOOLS

Tape measure, pencil, table saw or circular saw, jigsaw, drill and right-angle drill guide, level, carpenter's square, reciprocating saw with metal cutting blade, aviation snips, wire mesh, pliers, concrete mixer, 5-gal. buckets, shovel, wheelbarrow, wooden float, variable speed angle grinder with grinding pads, belt sander, automotive buffer.

MATERIALS

See photo, next page.

Kitchen Countertop

Cast concrete countertops have many unique characteristics. They are durable, heat resistant, and relatively inexpensive (if you make them yourself). But most of all, they are highly attractive and a great fit in contemporary kitchens or bathrooms.

A concrete countertop may be cast in place or formed offsite and installed like a natural stone countertop. Casting offsite makes more sense for most homeowners. In addition to keeping the mess and dust out of your living spaces, working in a garage or even outdoors lets you cast the countertops with the finished surface face down in the form. This way, if you do a careful job building the form, you can keep the grinding and polishing to a bare minimum. In some cases, you may even be able to simply remove the countertop from the form, flip it over, and install it essentially as is.

Planning a Concrete Countertop

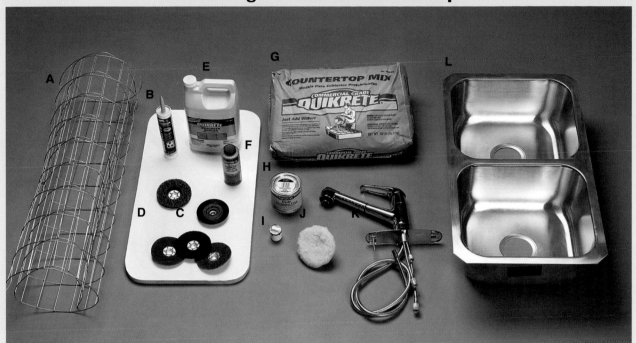

▶**The basic supplies needed to build your countertop form and cast the countertop** include: (A) welded wire mesh for reinforcement; (B) black or colored silicone caulk; (C) grinding and polishing pads; (D) Melamine coated particleboard for constructing the form; (E) concrete sealer; (F) coloring agent (liquid or powder); (G) bagged concrete countertop mix or high/ early mix rated for 5,000 psi; (H) paste wax; (I) knockout for faucet, if installing sink; (J) buffing bonnet for polisher; (K) faucet set; and (L) sink.

Custom Features

Concrete countertops are normally cast as flat slabs, but if you are willing to put a little more time and effort into it, there are many additional features you can create during the pour. A typical 3"-tall backsplash is challenging, but if you have room behind the faucet you can create a ¾"-tall backsplash shelf in the backsplash area. Or, if you search around for some additional information, you can learn how to cast a drainboard directly into the countertop surface. And there is practically no end to the decorative touches you can apply using pigments and inserts.

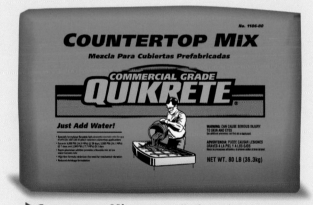

▶**Countertop Mix** is specially formulated concrete countertop mix designed for use in either precast or cast-in-place projects. Countertop mix contains additives that improve the workability, strength, and finish of the mix.

Estimating Concrete for Countertops

After you design your project and determine the actual dimensions, you'll need to estimate the amount of concrete you'll need. Concrete is measured by volume in cubic feet; multiply the length by the width and then by the thickness of the finished countertop for volume in cubic inches, then divide the sum by 1728 for cubic feet. For example, a countertop that will be 48" long x 24" deep x 3½" thick will require 2⅓ cu. ft. of mixed concrete (48 x 24 x 3.5 / 1728 = 2⅓) or four 80-lb. bags of countertop mix.

continued next page ▶

How to Cast a Concrete Countertop

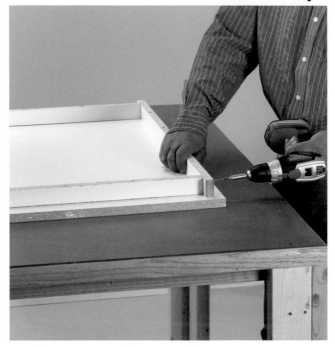

1 ■ **Make the form parts.** First, cut 1½"-wide strips of ¾" melamine-coated particleboard for the form sides. Cut the strips to length (26" and 81½" as shown here) and drill two countersunk pilot holes ³/₈" in from the ends of the front and back form sides. Assemble the strips into a frame by driving a 2" coarse wallboard screw at each pilot hole and into the mating ends of the end form strips.

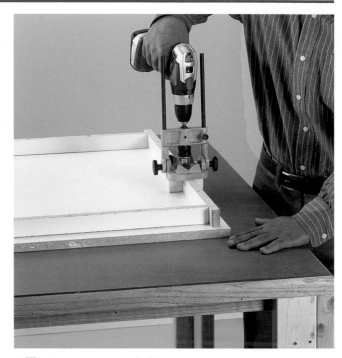

2 ■ **Use a power drill** mounted in a right-angle drill guide (or use a drill press) to drill ¼"-dia. guide holes for 3" deck screws at 6" intervals all the way through the tops of the form sides. Countersink the holes so the screw heads will be recessed slightly below the surface.

3 ■ **Attach the form sides to the base.** Center the melamine-strip frame pieces on the base, which should have the melamine coating face-up. Test the corners with a carpenter's square to make sure they're square. Drive one 3½" deck screw per form side near the middle. The screwheads should be slightly below the top edges of the forms. Check for square again, and continue driving the 3½" screws at 6" intervals through the pilot holes. Check for square frequently. Note: Do not drive any screws up through the underside of the form base—you won't be able to lift the countertop and access the screws when it's time to strip off the forms.

4 ■ **Make the sink knockout blanks** by stacking two pieces of ¾" melamine. The undermount sink we used requires a 20 x 31" knockout with corners that are rounded at a 2" radius. Cut two pieces of ¾"-thick MDF to 20 x 31" square using a table saw if you have one. With a compass, mark 2"-radius curves at each corner for trimming. Make the trim cuts with a jigsaw (as shown in photo). Cut just outside the trim line and sand up to it with a pad sander for a smooth curve.

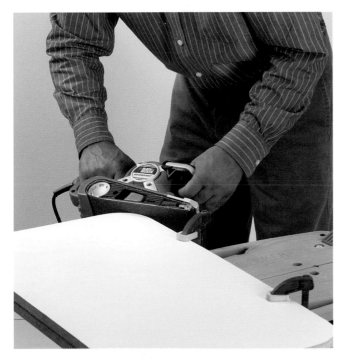

5 ■ **Shape the knockout.** Clamp the two pieces of melamine face-to-face for the knockout and gang sand the edges and corners so they're smooth and even. A belt sander on a stationary sanding station or an oscillating spindle sander works great for this. Don't oversand—this will cause the sink knockout to be too small.

6 ■ **Install the sink knockout.** Because gluing the faces together can add height to the knockout (and cause the concrete finishing tools to bang into it when they ride on the form tops), attach each blank directly to the layer below it using countersunk screws. Keep the edges aligned perfectly, especially if you're planning to install an undermount sink.

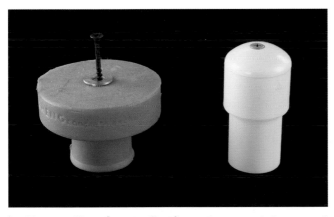

▶ **Faucet Knockouts Option:** If your sink faucet will not be mounted on the sink deck, you'll need to add a knockout to your form for the faucet hole (try and choose a single-handle faucet), according to the requirements of the faucet manufacturer. You can order knockouts from a concrete countertop supplies distributor, or you can create them with PVC pipe that has an outside diameter equal to the required faucet hole size. To anchor the PVC knockout, cover one end with a flat cap made for that size tubing. Drill a guide hole through the center of the cap so you can secure it with a screw. The top of the cap should be exactly flush with the form sides once it is installed. Before securing, position the knockout next to a form side and compare the heights. If the knockout is taller, file or sand the uncapped end so their lengths match.

7 ■ **Make the form watertight.** Seal exposed edges of the sink knockout with fast-drying polyurethane varnish, and then caulk the form once the varnish is dry. Run a very thin bead of colored silicone caulk (the coloring allows you to see where the caulk has been laid on the white melamine) in all the seams and then smooth carefully with a fingertip. In addition to keeping the wet concrete from seeping into gaps in the form, the caulk will create a slight roundover on the edges of the concrete. Caulk around the bottoms of the knockouts as well.

continued next page ▶

How to Cast a Concrete Countertop, continued

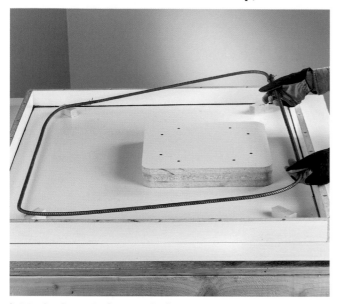

▶**Variation: Rebar Reinforcement.** If your counter-top is more than 2" thick, use #3 rebar (3/8" dia.) for the primary reinforcement. Do not use rebar on thinner countertops, as the rebar will necessarily be too close to the surface and can telegraph through. Bend the rebar to fit around the perimeter of the form using a rebar or conduit bender. The rebar needs to be at least 1" away from all edges (including knockouts) and 1" away from the top surface. Tie the ends of the rebar with wire and set it in the form on temporary 1" spacers.

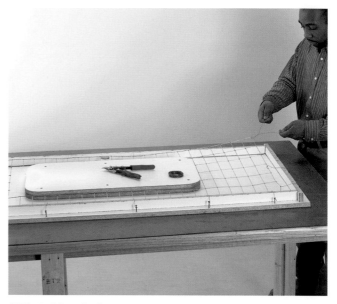

8 ■ **Add reinforcement.** Cut a piece of welded wire (also called re-wire) with a 4 x 4" grid so it's 2" smaller than the interior form dimensions. Make a cutout for the sink and faucet knockouts, making sure the re-wire does not come closer than 1" to any edge, surface, or knockout. Flatten the re-wire as best you can and then hang it with wires that are attached to the tops of the forms with screws (you'll remove the screws and cut the wires after the concrete is placed).

9 ■ **Clamp or screw the base** of the form to a sturdy workbench or table so the form cannot move during the critical finishing and curing stages. Check for level and insert shims between the worktop and the benchtop if needed for leveling. If you're concerned about mess, slip a sheet of 3-mil plastic on the floor under the workbench.

10 ■ **Blend** water with liquid cement color (if desired) in a 5-gal. bucket prior to adding to the mixer.

11■ **Slowly pour concrete** countertop mix into the mixer and blend for a minimum of 5 minutes. Properly mixed material will flow easily into molds. Add small amounts of water as necessary to achieve the desired consistency.

12■ **Fill the countertop form,** making sure to pack the concrete into corners and press it through the reinforcement. Overfill the form slightly.

13■ **Vibrate the form vigorously** as you work to settle concrete into all the voids. You can rent a concrete vibrator for this purpose, or simply strike the form repeatedly with a rubber mallet. If you have a helper and a sturdy floor and worktable, lift up and down on the ends of the table, bouncing it on the floor to cause vibrations (this is a very effective method if you can manage it safely). Make sure the table remains level when you're through.

14■ **Strike off excess concrete** from the form using a 2 x 4 drawn along the tops of the forms in a sawing motion. If voids are created, pack them with fresh concrete and re-strike. Do not overwork the concrete.

continued next page ▶

15 ▪ **Snip the wire ties** holding the re-wire mesh once you are certain you won't need to vibrate the form any further. Embed the cut ends attached to the re-wire below the concrete surface.

16 ▪ **Smooth the surface** of the concrete with a metal screeding tool, such as a length of angle iron or square metal tubing. Work slowly with a sawing motion, allowing the bleed water to fill in behind the screed. Since this surface will be the underside of the countertop, no further tooling is required. Cover the concrete with plastic and allow the concrete to dry undisturbed for three to five days.

17 ▪ **Remove the plastic covering** and then unscrew and remove the forms. Do not pry against the fresh concrete. In most cases, you'll need to cut apart the sink knockout to prevent damaging the countertop when removing it. Drill a starter hole and then carefully cut up to the edge of the knockout. Cut the knockout into chunks until you can remove it all. The edges of the concrete will be fragile, so be very careful.

18 ▪ **Flip the countertop** so the finished surface is exposed (you'll need a helper or two). Be extremely careful. The best technique is to roll the countertop onto an edge, position several shock-absorbing sleepers beneath it (rigid insulation board works very well), and then gently lower the countertop onto the sleepers.

19 ■ **To expose the aggregate** and create a very polished finish, grind the countertop surface. Use a series of increasingly fine grinding pads mounted on a shock-protected 5" angle grinder (variable speed). This is messy work, and can go on for hours to get the desired result. Rinse the surface regularly with clean water and make sure it stays wet during grinding. For a gleaming surface, mount still finer pads (up to 1,500 grit) on the grinder and wet-polish.

20 ■ **Clean and seal** the concrete with several coats of quality concrete sealer (one with penetrating and film-forming agents). For extra protection and a renewable finish, apply a coat of paste wax after the last coat of sealer dries.

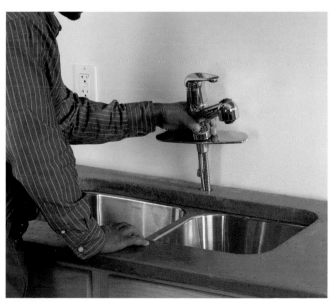

21 ■ **Mount the sink** (if undermount). Sinks are easier to install prior to attaching the countertop on the cabinet. Attach the sink according to the manufacturer's directions. Undermount sinks like this are installed with undermount clips and silicone adhesive. Self-rimming sinks likely will require some modifications to the mounting hardware (or at least you'll need to buy some extra-long screws) to accommodate the thickness of the countertop.

22 ■ **Install the countertop and hook up the plumbing.** Make sure the island cabinet is adequately reinforced and that as much plumbing as possible has been taken care of, then apply a thick bead of panel adhesive or silicone adhesive to the tops of the cabinets and stretchers. With at least one helper, lower the countertop onto the base and position it where you wish. Let the adhesive dry overnight before completing the sink and faucet hookups. ◆

Real glass block creates a beautiful, light-filled shower with low-maintenance walls that are far more elegant than a shower curtain or a flimsy glass-paned enclosure. Blocks are available with various patterns and textures for special light effects and different levels of privacy (inset).

QUIK-DATA

Cost	● ● ● ● ○
Skill	● ● ● ● ●
Time	● ● ● ● ○

TOOLS

4-ft. level, 2-ft. level, drill, mixing box or bucket, pointed (brick) trowel, rubber mallet, jointing tool, sponge, caulking gun.

MATERIALS

Glass blocks, shower base, wall ties, track, plastic glass block spacers, foam expansion strips, glass block mortar, flat 1x board, ⅜" and ¼" scrap wood, glass block panel anchors and reinforcing wire, 2" corrosion-resistant screws and washers, nonsag polyurethane sealant.

Glass Block Shower

Glass block has been a popular building material for nearly a century. Its unique combination of strength, transparency, and beauty make it the perfect solution for brightening a space without giving up privacy or security. And those same characteristics make glass block ideal for shower enclosures: it creates a washable, waterproof barrier that lets plenty of light into the shower while obscuring bathers from view.

Glass blocks come in several sizes, including 8" and 12" square blocks and 6 x 8" rectangular units. The standard thickness of blocks is about 4". As with brick and other masonry units, the nominal size of glass block includes an allowance for the mortar joints. An 8" square block actually measures 7 ¾" square, allowing for ¼"-thick mortar joints in the finished wall. Unlike standard masonry, glass block cannot be cut, so be sure to lay out your walls carefully, and do a dry run with the actual blocks (and using spacers to represent mortar joints) to make sure everything fits. Specialty blocks are available to let you turn corners, create curves, or finish the exposed ends or tops of walls.

QUIK-TIP

To give your glass block wall a colorful accent, spray paint the edges of the block prior to setting the blocks in place.

Planning a Glass Block Shower

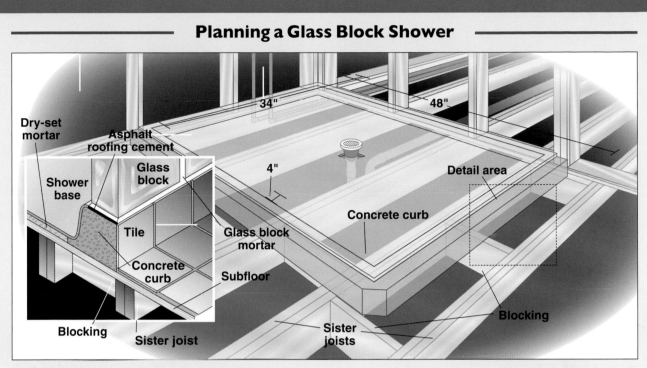

■ **Install water supply and drain pipes** before you begin the construction of the glass block shower. If you have to adjust the position of your base to fit the block wall, take this into account as you mark the location for the shower drain.

Reinforcement

■ **A glass block installation** must be anchored to a supporting wall stud on at least one end by means of panel anchors.

The block is mortared to its supporting base (see right) but not to the adjoining walls or ceiling —at these locations, foam expansion strips allow for movement between the adjoining structures.

Ladder-like reinforcement wire set into the mortar between alternating courses strengthens the block wall internally.

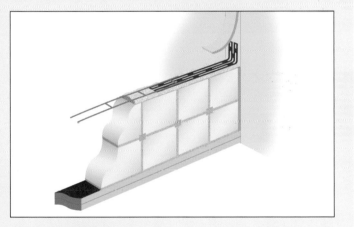

Glass Block Mortar Mix Calculator

Number of Blocks	6" (152 mm) Block # of Bags Required*	8" (203 mm) Block # of Bags Required*	12" (305 mm) # of Bags Required*
40	1	2	2
100	3	4	5
200	5	7	10
500	13	16	25

*50-lb (22.7 kg) bags

How to Build a Glass Block Shower Wall

1 ■ **Build the shower base with curb** (see illustration, previous page) or install a custom-order manufactured shower base with integral glass block curb following the manufacturer's directions. Here, a custom concrete curb and lined shower receptor have been installed.

2 ■ **Lay out the project area.** Using a 4 ft. level, draw a plumb line onto the wall to represent the inside (or outside) face of the glass block wall.

3 ■ **Dry-lay the first course** of glass blocks to establish a layout and so you can mark the height of the first course on the wall or walls you'll be fastening the glass block wall to.

4 ■ **Install wall ties** to the walls after every other course. Use wall anchors to secure the ties, and make sure the ties will reach past at least two glass block units in the layout.

5 ■ Add ³/₈"-thick foam expansion strips between the panel anchors on the supporting wall, cutting them to fit if necessary. You can use daubs of caulk or sealant behind the strips to keep them in place.

6 ■ Mix a batch of glass-block mortar following the product directions. A stiff mix is easiest to work with, so add water carefully to achieve the driest recommended consistency. (As you work, mix only enough mortar that you can use in about 30 minutes.)

7 ■ Spread a ³/₈"-thick full mortar bed along the curb for the first few blocks using a pointed trowel. Do not furrow the mortar. Set the first block into the mortar using spacers at the wall and curb. Tap the block with a rubber mallet or trowel handle to set it into the mortar.

8 ■ Butter one edge of the next block with a ³/₈"- to ½"-thick layer of mortar. Install the block using a T-spacer, and push it against the first block to create a ¼" mortar joint. Install the third block in the same manner.

continued next page ▶

9 ■ **Check the blocks** with a level as you work to make sure each one is plumb, level, and aligned with the other blocks. Tap the blocks with the mallet or trowel handle to adjust them. You can set a flat board across several blocks to check for level and make adjustments.

10 ■ **When the first course is complete,** fill any low spots at the tops of the joints with mortar. Set the spacers for the next course, then lay a full ⅜"-thick mortar bed. Install the second course of block, checking your work with a level.

Using Glass Block Spacers

■ **Full spacers help maintain joint spacing** where four glass blocks meet. To use spacers where blocks adjoin a wall, ceiling, or curb, break off the side tabs, then trim off two of the spacer legs to create T-spacers. For the outside corners of a wall, trim off four legs to create L-spacers.

11■ **Lay down a half-thickness mortar bed** for the third course, and then set the first panel anchor into the mortar. Cut a length of glass block reinforcement track to span the wall, and set it into the mortar, overlapping the anchor by 6". Add the other half of the mortar over the wire and anchors, and install the next course of block.

12■ **Clean up the joints.** When the mortar in the lower courses is hard enough to resist light finger pressure (typically within 30 minutes), twist off the T-spacer tabs (inset photo) and pack mortar into the voids. Smooth the joints with a glass block jointing tool. Fill in low spots with mortar and remove excess and spilled mortar with a soft brush or damp sponge, rinsing frequently.

13■ **Clean as you go.** As you complete each row (about 30 minutes after tooling the joints), clean and smooth the joints with a wet tile setter's sponge, rinsing frequently. After the wall is complete, remove the cloudy residue from the blocks using a clean, dry cloth, and then buff with a piece of scrap carpeting.

QUIK-TIP

Use a dry 4 x 4" piece of carpet to clean the glass block surface. The carpet will lift the cement without smearing.

14■ **Let the mortar cure** for at least 24 hours, and then seal around the glass block wall(s) with silicone sealant or non-sag polyurethane sealant. Apply a sealant to the mortar joints, if desired, following the manufacturer's directions. ◆

Acid-stained Concrete Floor

Etching stain can have a dramatic effect on plain concrete, transforming a basic gray slab into a richly colored finished floor. QUIKRETE® Etching Stain and Etching Stain High-Gloss Sealer make it easy to color and protect any type of concrete floor—from basement slabs and interior finish floors to garages, patios, and walkways.

Applied as a liquid, etching stain chemically reacts with minerals in concrete to create a permanent finish. Because concrete is porous, the coloring is attractively multitoned, similar to the warm, natural hues of weathered stone or earthen tile. Coating your stained floor with a clear sealer adds a tough protective layer that helps resist unwanted stains and enhances the depth of color.

For new concrete, you can apply stain and topcoat anytime after 60 days. For existing concrete surfaces, a thorough cleaning with trisodium phosphate (TSP) or baking soda will help ensure even absorption of the stain and a strong bond with the sealer. Make sure to seal the stain within 24 hours of staining as the salts can oxidize, creating an unfavorable sealing condition.

Work safely. Etching stain contains acid. To protect yourself from fumes and skin contact, wear pants and a long-sleeve shirt, acid-resistant boots and gloves, splash-resistant safety goggles, and a respirator that filters hydrochloric acid. Keep the work area well ventilated at all times.

QUIK-TIP

Make sure the floor is clean. Remove all residue of grease, oils, paint, wax, and sealants using Bond-Lok cleaner-etcher-degreaser. Wash the floor thoroughly with water and note any areas where water beads on the surface. Clean these areas again until water can be absorbed into the concrete.

How to Stain & Seal a Concrete Floor

1■ **Thoroughly clean the entire floor** (see opposite page). Use painter's tape and plastic sheeting to protect any areas that won't be stained, as well as surrounding walls and other surfaces. Test the spray of your garden sprayer using water: it should deliver a wide, even mist.

2■ **Dampen the floor with water** using a garden sprayer. Mop up any pooled water, but make sure the entire floor is damp. Load sprayer with stain, and then apply the stain evenly in a circular motion until the concrete is saturated. Let the floor dry.

3■ **Remove the etching residue** by soaking the floor with water and scrubbing vigorously with a stiff-bristled brush. As you work, clean up the liquid with a wet/dry vacuum. Dispose of the waste liquid safely, according to local regulations.

4■ **When the floor has dried** completely (at least 18 to 24 hours), begin applying the sealer along the edges and in any hard-to-reach areas, using a paintbrush.

5■ **Using a ³/₈" nap roller,** apply the sealer in 2 x 6-ft. sections, maintaining a wet edge to prevent lap marks. If the sealer rapidly sinks into the concrete, apply a second coat after 2 hours. Let the floor dry for 18 to 24 hours before allowing light foot traffic and 72 hours before heavy use. ◆

Concrete &
MASONRY REPAIRS

Concrete, brick, and stucco are among the world's most durable and low-maintenance building materials, but they may need occasional upkeep and repairs to look and perform their best. Because masonry is very rigid (and sometimes because neighboring elements like wood and soil are not), cracking is one of the most common forms of damage in masonry structures and surfaces. Concrete slabs are almost guaranteed to crack; control joints are cut into large slabs simply to help direct where cracks occur, not to prevent them from occurring. However, unless there's a problem with the underlying soil or gravel base, most cracks have little or no effect on the slab's performance, and repairs are often long-lasting.

Brick structures, including walls and brick veneer siding, commonly suffer from deterioration of the mortar. By design, mortar is softer than brick, and this means it's more prone to weathering over time. The standard repair for weathered and missing mortar is tuck-pointing. Isolated damage to individual bricks is usually corrected by replacing the bricks.

When used as house siding, stucco often becomes damaged due to problems with the underlying wall structure, such as shifting or shrinkage of wood framing or moisture trapped in the wall cavity or behind the siding. Repairs to the stucco layer itself are usually straightforward and long-lasting, but be sure to solve any underlying problems (especially moisture, rot, and structural issues) before making repairs.

In This Chapter

- **Repairing Concrete**

- **Patching Cracks**

- **Quick Fixes for Wet Walls**

- **Renewing an Old Concrete Slab**

- **Brick Repairs**

- **Repairing Stucco**

QUIK-DATA

Cost	●
Skill	●
Time	●

TOOLS

Trowels, drill with masonry-grinding disc, circular saw with masonry-cutting blade, cold chisel, hand maul, paintbrush, screed board, float.

MATERIALS

Scrap lumber, vegetable oil or commercial release agent, hydraulic cement, bonding agent, vinyl-reinforced patching compound, sand-mix concrete, concrete fortifier, plastic sheeting.

Repairing Concrete

Large and small holes are treated differently when repairing concrete. The best product for filling in smaller holes (less than ½" deep) is vinyl-reinforced concrete patcher. Reinforced repair products should be applied only in layers that are ¼" thick or less. For deeper holes, use sand-mix concrete with an acrylic fortifier, which can be applied in layers up to 2" thick.

Patches in concrete will be more effective if you create clean, backward-angled cuts around the damaged area, to create a stronger bond. For extensive cutting of damaged concrete, it's best to score the concrete first with a circular saw equipped with a masonry blade. Use a chisel and maul to complete the job.

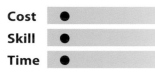

QUIK-TIP

Use fast-set repair mortar or quick-setting cement with acrylic fortifier for repairing holes and chip-outs in vertical surfaces. Because they set up in just a few minutes, these products can be shaped to fill holes without the need for forms.

How to Patch a Small Hole

1■ Cut out around the damaged area with a masonry-grinding disc mounted on a portable drill (or use a hammer and stone chisel). The cuts should bevel about 15° away from the center of the damaged area. Chisel out any loose concrete within the repair area. Always wear gloves and eye protection.

2■ Dampen the repair area with clean water and then fill it with vinyl concrete patcher. Pack the material in with a trowel, allowing it to crown slightly above the surrounding surface. Then, feather the edges so the repair is smooth and flat. Protect the repair from foot traffic for at least one day and three days from vehicle traffic.

How to Patch a Large Hole

1 ◼ Use a hammer and chisel or a heavy floor scraper to remove all material that is loose or shows any deterioration. Thoroughly clean the area with a hose and nozzle or a pressure washer.

▶**OPTION:** Make beveled cuts around the perimeter of the repair area with a circular saw and masonry-cutting blade. The bevels should slant down and away from the damage to create a "key" for the repair material.

2 ◼ Mix concrete patching compound according to the manufacturer's instructions, and then trowel it neatly into the damage area, which should be dampened before the patching material is placed. Overfill the damage area slightly.

3 ◼ Smooth and feather the repair with a steel trowel so it is even with the surrounding concrete surface. Finish the surface of the repair material to blend with the existing surface. For example, use a whisk broom to recreate a broomed finish. Protect the repair from foot traffic for at least one day and three days from vehicle traffic. ◆

Concrete repair caulk can be forced into small cracks to keep them from expanding. Smooth the caulk after application.

Patching Cracks

The materials and methods you should use for repairing cracks in concrete depend on the location and size of the crack. For small cracks (less than ½" wide) you can use concrete repair caulk for a quick aesthetic fix. Sanded acrylic repair caulks do a good job of matching the color and texture of concrete and stucco surfaces. Larger cracks require concrete repair materials that are fast-setting and high-strength polymer modified compounds that significantly increase the bonding properties and long-term durability of the concrete repair. Cracks that are a result of continual slab movement often cannot be repaired with a rigid concrete repair material. These cracks should be repaired with flexible polyurethane sealants that will elongate with the movement of the flexible concrete crack.

Recommended Crack Preparation

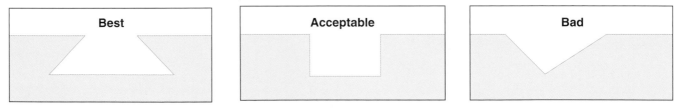

| Best | Acceptable | Bad |

▶ **The best way to repair cracks** in concrete is to enlarge the crack first by chiseling a keyway along the crack path with a cold chisel. The best holding power for the new patch material is achieved if you chisel in a dovetail shape. A square keyway will also work. A V-shaped keyway will ultimately lead to failure of the repair.

How to Repair Horizontal Cracks

1 ▪ **Prepare the crack** for the repair materials by knocking away any loose or deteriorating material and beveling the edges down and outward with a cold chisel. Sweep or vacuum the debris and thoroughly dampen the repair area. Do not allow any water to pool, however.

2 ▪ **Mix the repair product** to fill the crack according to the manufacturer's instructions. Here, a fast-setting cement repair product with acrylic fortifier is being used. Trowel the product into the crack, overfilling slightly. With the edge of the trowel, trim the excess material and feather it so it is smooth and the texture matches the surrounding surface. ◆

How to Repair Vertical Cracks

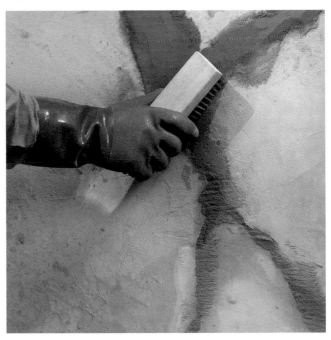

1 ▪ **Prepare the crack** for repair as with a horizontal crack (step 1, above) and then fill the crack with fast-setting repair mortar. The mixture should have a fairly dry consistency so it does not run out of the crack. Overfill the crack slightly and allow the repair material to set up.

2 ▪ **Shape or trim** the concrete repair product so it is even with surrounding surface and the textures match. If the material has set too much and is difficult to work, try using a wire attachment on a power drill. ◆

Although most water problems in basements are not caused by cracks in the foundation wall, a large crack should be repaired immediately, especially in a damp basement. To repair it, create a dovetail-shaped keyway with a cold chisel and maul, and then fill the crack with hydraulic repair cement (this product actually cures and hardens when it contacts water).

QUIK-DATA

Cost	● ●
Skill	● ● ●
Time	● ●

TOOLS

Wire brush, stiff-bristle paintbrush, sponge, square-end trowel.

MATERIALS

Hydraulic water stop cement, heavy-duty masonry coating, surface bonding cement.

Quick Fixes for Wet Walls

Failing gutters, broken or leaking pipes, condensation, and seepage are the most common causes of basement moisture. If allowed to persist, dampness can cause major damage to concrete basement walls. There are several effective ways to seal and protect the walls. If condensation is the source of the problem, check first that your clothes dryer is properly vented, and install a dehumidifier. If water is seeping in through small cracks or holes in the walls, repair damaged gutters and leaky pipes, and check the grade of the soil around your foundation. Once you've addressed the problem at its source, create a waterproof seal over openings in the basement walls. To stop occasional seepage, coat the walls with masonry sealer. For more frequent seepage, seal the openings and resurface the walls with a water-resistant masonry coating. Heavy-duty coatings, such as surface bonding cement (opposite page) are best for very damp conditions. Thinner brush-on coatings are also available. For chronic seepage, ask a contractor to install a baseboard gutter and drain system.

Remember: To prevent long-term damage, it's necessary to identify the source of the moisture and make repairs both inside and outside your home, so moisture no longer penetrates foundation walls.

Tips for Inspecting & Sealing Basement Walls

■ **Paint that is peeling off** basement walls usually indicates water seepage from outside that is trapped between the walls and the paint.

■ **Tape a square** of aluminum foil to a masonry wall to identify high moisture levels. Check the foil after 24 hours. Beads of water on top of the foil indicate high humidity in the room. Beads of water underneath suggest water seepage through the wall from outside.

■ **To control minor seepage** through porous concrete and masonry, seal walls with a cement-based masonry sealer. Clean the walls and prepare by adding acrylic fortifier to heavy-duty masonry coating. Dampen the walls and apply masonry coating to the walls (including all masonry joints) with a stiff masonry brush in a circular motion.

■ **Resurface heavily cracked masonry walls** with a water-resistant masonry coating, such as fiber-reinforced surface bonding cement with acrylic fortifier. Clean and dampen the walls according to the coating manufacturer's instructions, then fill large cracks and holes with the coating. Finally, plaster a ¼" layer of the coating on the walls using a finishing trowel. Specially formulated heavy-duty masonry coatings are available for very damp conditions.

AFTER

BEFORE

Concrete resurfacer offers an easy, inexpensive solution for renewing patios, driveways, paths, steps, and other concrete surfaces that have become chipped and flaked with age.

QUIK-DATA

Cost	● ●
Skill	● ●
Time	● ●

TOOLS

3,500 psi pressure washer, steel concrete finishing trowel, long-handled squeegee, ½" drill with paddle mixer, 5-gallon bucket, duct tape or backer rod, stiff-bristle broom.

MATERIALS

Concrete resurfacer.

Renewing an Old Concrete Slab

Over time, exposed concrete surfaces can start to show a lot of wear. Weather, hard use, and problems with the initial pour and finishing are among the most common causes of surface blemishes. But despite a shabby appearance, old concrete is often structurally sound and can last for many more years. So instead of breaking up and replacing an old slab, you can easily renew its surface with concrete resurfacer. With the simple application your concrete will have a freshly poured look and a protective surface layer that's typically stronger than the slab itself.

Concrete resurfacer is suitable for any size of slab, outdoors or indoors. You can also apply it to vertical surfaces to put a fresh face on steps, curbs, and exposed patio edges. Depending on the condition of the old surface, the new layer can range in thickness from ¹⁄₁₆ to ¼". For a smooth finish, spread the resurfacer with a squeegee or trowel. For a textured or nonslip surface, you can broom the surface before it dries or use a masonry brush for smaller applications.

How to Renew an Old Slab

1 ▇ Thoroughly clean the entire project area. If necessary, remove all oil and greasy or waxy residue using a concrete cleaner and scrub brush. Water beading on the surface indicates residue that could prevent proper adhesion with the resurfacer; clean these areas again as needed.

2 ▇ Wash the concrete with a pressure washer. Set the washer at 3,500 psi, and hold the fan-spray tip about 3" from the surface or as recommended by the washer manufacturer. Remove standing water.

3 ▇ Fill sizeable pits and spalled areas using a small batch of concrete resurfacer—mix about 5 pints of water per 40-lb. bag of resurfacer for a trowelable consistency. Repair cracks or broken slab edges as shown on pages 116 to 119. Smooth the repairs level with the surrounding surface, and let them harden.

4 ▇ On a large project, section off the slab into areas no larger than 100 sq. ft. It's easiest to delineate sections along existing control joints. On all projects, cover or seal off all control joints with duct tape, foam backer rod, or weatherstripping to prevent resurfacer from spilling into the joints.

continued next page ▶

6 ■ **Saturate the work area** with water, then use a squeegee to remove any standing water. Pour the mix of concrete resurfacer onto the center of the repair area or first repair section.

5 ■ **Mix the desired quantity** of concrete resurfacer with water, following the mixing instructions. Work the mix with a ½" drill and a mixing paddle for 5 minutes to achieve a smooth, pourable consistency. If necessary, add water sparingly until the mix will pour easily and spread well with a squeegee.

QUIK-TIP

For improved color consistency, apply a thin slurry coat of concrete resurfacer to seal the concrete substrate. An additional coat can be applied after 2 hours.

7 ■ **Spread the resurfacer** with the squeegee, using a scrubbing motion to make sure all depressions are filled. Then, spread it into a smooth, consistent layer. If desired, broom the surface for a nonslip finish (opposite page). You can also tool the slab edges with a concrete edger within 20 minutes of application. Let the resurfacer cure. *Tip: Resurface outdoor projects when the temperature will stay above 50°F for 8 hours and the surface won't freeze for at least 24 hours. Cover the area only if necessary to protect it from rain in the first 6 hours of curing (this may affect surface appearance and uniformity). During extreme wind or sun conditions, moist-cure the surface with a water fog-spray twice daily for 24 to 48 hours after application. Let resurfacer cure for 6 hours before allowing foot traffic and 24 hours before vehicle traffic (wait longer during cold weather).* ◆

Options for Resurfacer Finishes

▶**For thicker resurfacing,** simply add more layers of resurfacer as needed. Wait until the surface can support foot traffic—typically 2 to 6 hours—before applying the next coat.

▶**Nonslip broomed finish:** Within 5 minutes of applying the resurfacer, drag a clean fine-bristled push broom across the surface. Pull the broom backward in a straight line, moving across the entire area without stopping. Repeat in parallel rows until the entire surface is textured.

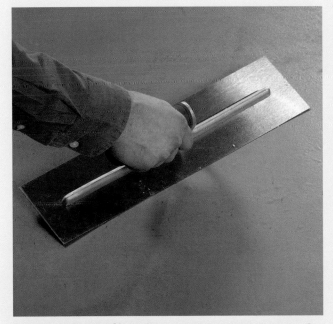

▶ **Trowel application:** A trowel is handy for resurfacing small areas. Use a stiffer mix for troweling—approximately 5 pints of water per 40-lb. bag of dry mix. Spread and smooth the resurfacer with a steel concrete-finishing trowel.

▶ **Brush application:** Resurface curbs, step risers, and slab edges using a masonry brush. Mix a workably stiff batch of resurfacer, and apply it evenly over the repair area. Finishing the surface with short brush strokes produces a mottled appearance; straight, continuous strokes create a broomed look.

Make timely repairs to brick and block structures. Tuck-pointing deteriorated mortar joints is a common repair that, like other types of repair, improves the appearance of the structure or surface and helps prevent further damage.

TOOLS

Raking tool, mortar hawk, tuck-pointer, jointing tool, bricklayer's hammer, mason's trowel, mason's or stone chisel, pointing trowel, drill with masonry disc and bit, stiff-bristle brush.

MATERIALS

Mortar (Type S or N), gravel, scrap of metal flashing, replacement bricks or blocks, mortar repair caulk.

Brick Repairs

The most common brick wall repair is tuck-pointing, which is the process of replacing failed mortar joints with fresh mortar. Tuck-pointing is a highly useful repair skill for any homeowner to possess. It can be used to repair walls, chimneys, brick veneer, or any other structure where the bricks or blocks are bonded with mortar.

Minor cosmetic repairs can be attempted on any type of wall, from freestanding garden walls to block foundations. Filling minor cracks with caulk or repair compound, and patching popouts or chips are good examples of minor repairs. Consult a professional before attempting any major repairs, like replacing brick or blocks, or rebuilding a structure—especially if you are dealing with a load-bearing structure.

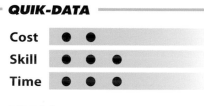

QUIK-TIP

Sanded-acrylic mortar repair caulk will give the appearance of mortar in texture and color.

How to Tuck-Point Mortar Joints

1■ Clean out loose or deteriorated mortar to a depth of ¼ to ¾". Use a mortar raking tool (top) first, then switch to a masonry chisel and a hammer (bottom) if the mortar is stubborn. Clear away all loose debris, and dampen the surface with water before applying fresh mortar.

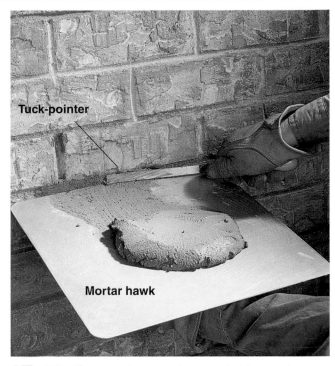

Tuck-pointer

Mortar hawk

2■ Mix the mortar to a firm workable consistency; add tint if necessary. Load mortar onto a mortar hawk, then push it into the horizontal joints with a tuck-pointer. Apply mortar in ¼ to ½" thick layers, and let each layer dry for 30 minutes before applying another. Fill the joints until the mortar is flush with the face of the brick or block.

3■ After the final layer of mortar is applied, smooth the joints with a jointing tool that matches the profile of the old mortar joints. Tool the horizontal joints first. Let the mortar dry until it is crumbly, then brush off the excess mortar with a stiff-bristle brush.

4■ Apply mortar repair caulk with firm pressure filling the mortar joint from back to front in multiple layers. Use the square applicator tip or a jointing tool to smooth the joint. ◆

How to Replace a Damaged Brick

1■ **Score the damaged brick** so it will break apart more easily for removal. Use a drill with a masonry-cutting disc to score lines along the surface of the brick and in the mortar joints surrounding the brick.

2■ **Use a mason's chisel and hammer** to break apart the damaged brick along the scored lines. Rap sharply on the chisel with the hammer, being careful not to damage surrounding bricks. *Tip: Save fragments to use as a color reference when you shop for replacement bricks.*

3■ **Chisel out any remaining mortar** in the cavity, then brush out debris with a stiff-bristle or wire brush to create a clean surface for the new mortar. Rinse the surface of the repair area with water.

4■ **Mix the mortar for the repair,** and tint if needed to match old mortar. Use a pointing trowel to apply a 1"-thick layer of mortar at the bottom and sides of the cavity.

5 ■ **Dampen the replacement brick** slightly, then apply mortar to the ends and top of the brick. Fit the brick into the cavity and rap it with the handle of the trowel until the face is flush with the surrounding bricks. If needed, press additional mortar into the joints with a pointing trowel.

6 ■ **Scrape away excess mortar** with a masonry trowel, then smooth the joints with a jointing tool that matches the profile of the surrounding mortar joints. Let the mortar set until crumbly, then brush the joints to remove excess mortar. ◆

Tips for Removing & Replacing Several Bricks

▶ **For walls with extensive damage**, remove bricks from the top down, one row at a time, until the entire damaged area is removed. Replace bricks using the techniques shown above and in the section on building with brick and block. Caution: Do not dismantle load-bearing brick structures like foundation walls—consult a professional mason for these repairs.

▶ **For walls with internal damaged areas**, remove only the damaged section, keeping the upper layers intact if they are in good condition. Do not remove more than four adjacent bricks in one area—if the damaged area is larger, it will require temporary support, which is a job for a professional mason.

Fill thin cracks in stucco walls with stucco repair caulk. Overfill the crack with caulk and feather until it's flush with the stucco. Allow the caulk to set, then paint it to match the stucco. Stucco caulk stays semiflexible, preventing further cracking.

Repairing Stucco

Although stucco siding is very durable, it can be damaged, and over time it can crumble or crack. The directions given below work well for patching small areas less than 2 sq. ft. For more extensive damage, the repair is done in layers, as shown on the opposite page.

Fill thin cracks in stucco walls with a sanded acyrlic stucco caulk. Overfill the crack with caulk and feather until it's flush with the stucco. Allow the caulk to set, then paint it to match the stucco. Masonry caulk stays semiflexible, preventing further cracking.

Premixed stucco patch works well for small holes, cracks, or surface defects. Repairs to large damaged areas often require the application of multiple layers of base coat stucco and a finish coat stucco. Matching the stucco texture may require some practice.

How to Patch Small Areas

1 ▪ **Remove loose material** from the repair area using a wire brush. Use the brush to clean away rust from any exposed metal lath, then apply a coat of metal primer to the lath.

2 ▪ **Apply premixed stucco** patch compound to the repair area, slightly overfilling the hole using a putty knife or trowel.

3 ▪ **Smooth the repair** with a putty knife or trowel, feathering the edges to blend into the surrounding surface. Use a whisk broom or trowel to duplicate the original texture. Let the patch dry for several days, then touch it up with masonry paint. ◆

How to Patch Large Areas

1 ■ **Make a starter hole** with a drill and masonry bit, then use a masonry chisel and hammer to chip away stucco in the repair area. Cut self-furring metal lath to size and attach it to the sheathing using roofing nails. Overlap pieces by 2". If the patch extends to the base of the wall, attach a metal stop bead at the bottom. Note: Wear safety glasses and a particle mask or respirator when cutting stucco.

2 ■ **Apply a ⅜"-thick layer of base coat stucco** directly to the metal lath. Push the stucco into the mesh until it fills the gap between the mesh and the sheathing. Score horizontal grooves into the wet surface using a scratching tool. Let the stucco cure for up to two days, misting it with water every 2 to 4 hours.

3 ■ **Apply a second, smooth layer** of stucco after the first coat has become sufficiently firm to hold the second coat without sagging. Build up the stucco to within ¼" of the original surface. Let the patch cure for up to two days, misting every 2 to 4 hours.

4 ■ **Combine finish coat stucco mix** with just enough water for the mixture to hold its shape. Dampen the patch area, then apply the finish coat to match the original surface. Dampen the patch occasionally. Let it cure for 7 days before painting with acrylic or water-based paint, and 28 days for oil-based. ◆

Tools &
TECHNIQUES

This section includes background information and detailed instructions for working with poured concrete, brick, and concrete block. You'll also see many of the masonry tools called for in the projects in this book. Aside from the special hand tools used for finishing concrete or for cutting and laying brick or block, there isn't a lot of extra equipment to buy or rent for most projects. You may already own many of the basic tools for site preparation and form building: basic carpentry tools like saws, levels, a tape measure, and squares; and landscaping tools like a wheelbarrow, a rake, shovels and other digging tools. Most of the specialty tools you'll need are inexpensive enough to buy, even though you'll use them only for masonry projects. Bigger items like a power mixer and power tamper are commonly available for rent.

The best place to shop for tools and materials depends on your project. For bagged concrete, mortar, stucco mixes, sand and gravel, and repair materials as well as colorants and other additives, most home centers will carry what you need. Big retailers also sell concrete finishing tools, bricklaying tools, concrete tube forms, and smaller quantities of rebar and other concrete reinforcing materials. If you can't find the right items at a home center, visit a brick or concrete materials supplier (look in the phone book under "Brick," "Concrete Reinforcements," or "Mason Equipment & Supplies").

━━━ In This Chapter ━━━

- **Working with Poured Concrete**

- **Mixing Concrete**

- **Placing & Finishing Concrete**

- **Working with Mortar**

- **Mixing & Placing Mortar**

The basic ingredients of concrete are the same, whether the concrete is mixed from scratch, purchased premixed, or delivered by a ready-mix company. Portland cement is the bonding agent. Sand and a combination of aggregates add volume and strength to the mix. Water activates the cement and is used in the hardening process called hydration. By varying the ratios of the ingredients, professionals can create concrete with special properties that are suited for specific situations.

Working with Poured Concrete

Durable, versatile, and economical, poured concrete can be shaped and finished into a wide variety of surfaces and structures throughout your home and yard. Decorative surfaces and unique appearances can be produced with exposed aggregate, tints and stains, and special stamping tools.

Good preparation means fewer delays at critical moments and leaves you free to focus on placing and smoothing the concrete—not on staking loose forms or locating misplaced tools. Before beginning to mix or pour the concrete, make sure the forms are sturdy enough to stand up to the weight and pressure that will be exerted on them and that they are staked and braced well. Forms that are taller than 4 or 5 inches

should be tied with wire. The joints on the forms should be tight enough that the bleed water doesn't run through them.

One of the most difficult aspects of finishing concrete is recognizing when it's ready. Many people try to rush the process, with disappointing results. Wait until the bleed water disappears and the concrete has hardened somewhat before floating the surface. A good rule of thumb is when the footprints you leave are light enough that you can no longer identify the type of shoes you are wearing, the concrete is ready to be worked.

Tools for Concrete Projects

■ **Safety tools and equipment** include particle masks, gloves, safety glasses, and tall rubber boots. Wear protective gear and gloves when handling dry or mixed concrete. These mixes are very alkaline and can burn eyes and skin.

■ **Mixing and pouring tools** include masonry hoe and mortar box for mixing small amounts of concrete; garden hose and bucket for delivering and measuring water; and power mixer for mixing medium-sized (between ½ and 3 cu. ft.) loads of concrete.

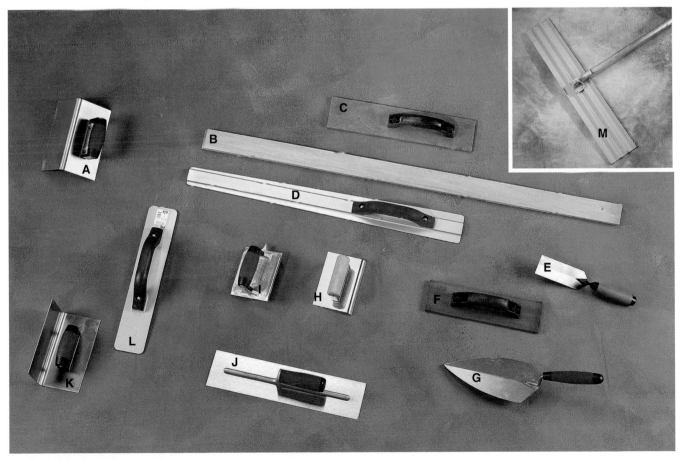

■ **Finishing tools** include outside corner tool (A); screed board (B) for striking off placed concrete; long wood float (C); aluminum darby (D) for smoothing concrete; margin trowel (E) for finishing; standard-length wood float (F); London trowel (G); edger (H) for shaping and forming edges; groover (I) for forming control joints; steel trowel (J); inside corner tool (K); magnesium float (L); and long-handled bull float (M) for smoothing large slabs.

Materials for Concrete Projects

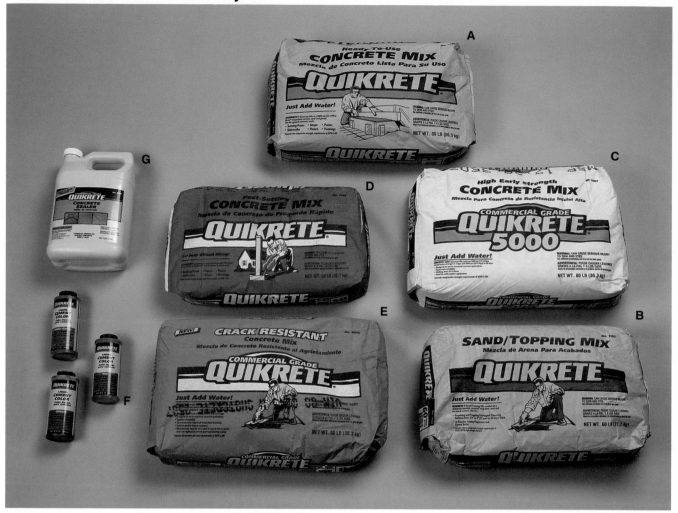

■ **Concrete mix,** usually sold in 40-, 60- or 80-lb. bags, contains all the components of concrete. You simply add water, mix, and place the concrete. Several varieties are offered at most building centers. The most common are: general-purpose 4,000 psi mix (A), which is the least expensive and is suitable for most do-it-yourself and contractor projects; sand mix (B) contains no large aggregate and is used for shallow pours, such as pouring overlays less than 2" thick (that's why it's sometimes called topping mix); high-early strength mix (C) contains agents and additives that cause it to strengthen quickly, achieving 5,000 psi after 28 days. This mix is particularly appropriate for patios, driveway aprons, and concrete countertops. Other common bagged concrete varieties include fast-setting concrete mix (D) with initial set times under 40 minutes and used for setting posts without mixing; and crack resistant concrete mix (E), a fiber-reinforced concrete mix with improved freeze-thaw durability characteristics.

■ **Concrete additives** include liquid colorant (F) that is added to the mix to produce vividly colored concrete; and acrylic sealer (G) to promote curing by retaining water in freshly placed concrete.

■ **Materials for subbases and forms** include compactible gravel (A) to improve drainage beneath the poured concrete structure; asphalt-impregnated fiberboard (B) to keep concrete from bonding with adjoining structures and to allow for expansion and contraction of concrete slabs; lumber (C) and 3" screws (D) for building forms; stakes (E) for holding the forms in place; and vegetable oil (F) or a commercial release agent to make it easier to remove the forms.

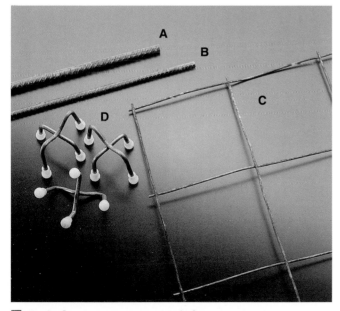

■ **Reinforcement materials:** Metal rebar (A & B), available in sizes ranging from #2 ($1/8$" dia.) to #5 ($5/8$" dia.) for reinforcing concrete slabs, like sidewalks, and in masonry walls. Wire mesh (C) (sometimes called remesh) is most common in 6 × 6" grids. For broad surfaces, like patios; bolsters (D) for suspending rebar and wire mesh.

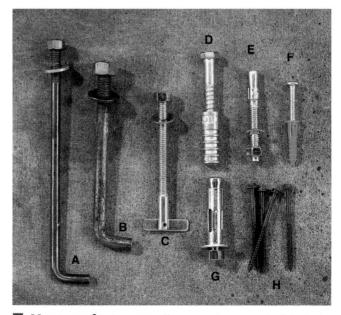

■ **Masonry fasteners** allow you to mount objects to concrete and other masonry surfaces. It is most effective to embed the fasteners in fresh concrete so that it cures around the hardware. Examples include J-bolt with nuts and washers (A, B); removable T-anchor (C); metal sleeve anchor (D); compression sleeves (E, G); light-duty plastic anchor sleeve (F); self-tapping coated steel screws (H).

Too dry   Too wet   Correct

A good mixture is crucial to any successful concrete project. Properly mixed concrete is damp enough to form in your hand when you squeeze, and dry enough to hold its shape. If the mixture is too dry, the aggregate will be difficult to work, and will not smooth out easily to produce an even, finished appearance. A wet mixture will slide off the trowel and may cause cracking and other defects in the finished surface.

QUIK-DATA

Cost	●
Skill	●
Time	●

TOOLS

Power mixer, wheelbarrow or mortar box, hoe, 5-gal. bucket, safety glasses, gloves, particle mask.

MATERIALS

Concrete mix, water, additives as desired.

Mixing Concrete

When mixing concrete on-site, purchase bags of dry premixed concrete and simply add water. Follow the instructions carefully and take note of exactly how much water you add so the concrete will be uniform from one batch to the next. For smaller projects, mix the concrete in a wheelbarrow or mortar box. For larger projects, rent or buy a power mixer. Be aware that most power mixers should not be filled more than half full.

When mixing concrete, the more water you add, the weaker the concrete will become. Mix the concrete only until all of the dry ingredients are moistened. Don't overwork it; three to five minutes should be enough.

Concrete Mix Calculator

Square Feet (M²)	2 (0.2)	5 (0.5)	10 (0.9)	25 (2.3)	50 (4.7)	100 (9.3)
4" (102 mm) thick slabs - # of 80-lb (36.3 kg) bags	1	3	6	14	28	56
6" (153 mm) thick slabs - # of 80-lb (36.3 kg) bags	2	5	9	21	42	84

All yields are approximate and do not allow for waste or uneven substrate, etc.

How to Mix Concrete

1 ■ **Empty premixed concrete bags** into a mortar box or wheelbarrow. Form a hollow in the mound of dry mix, and then pour water into the hollow. Start with ¾ of the expected water amount per 80-lb bag.

2 ■ **Work with a hoe,** continuing to add water until a good consistency is achieved. Clear out any dry pockets from the corners. Do not overwork the mix. Also, keep track of how much water you use in the first batch so you will have a reliable recipe for subsequent batches. ◆

Using a Power Mixer

1 ■ **Fill a bucket** with ¾ gal. of water for each 80-lb bag of concrete you will use in the batch (for most power mixers, three bags is workable). Pour in half the water. Before you start power-mixing, review the operating instructions carefully.

2 ■ **Add all of the dry ingredients,** then mix for 1 minute. Pour in water as needed until the proper consistency is achieved, and mix for 3 to 5 minutes. Pivot the mixing drum to empty the concrete into a wheelbarrow. Rinse out the drum immediately. ◆

Cost ● ● ●

Skill ● ● ●

Time ● ● ●

TOOLS

Wheelbarrow, hoe, spade, hammer, mason's trowel, float, groover, edger.

MATERIALS

Concrete, 2 × 4 lumber, mixing container, water.

Placing & Finishing Concrete

Placing concrete involves pouring it into forms, then leveling and smoothing it with special masonry tools. Once the surface is smooth and level, control joints are cut and the edges are rounded. Special attention to detail in these steps will result in a professional appearance.

QUIK-TIP

Dampen gravel subbases prior to placement of concrete to allow proper curing. Hot or dry subbases will draw water away from the concrete mix.

Tips for Pouring Concrete

▶**Mix concrete** directly in a wheelbarrow or transfer it to a wheelbarrow from a power mixer, and then place the concrete simply by tipping the wheelbarrow. If you are pouring a formed slab, lay out planking so your wheelbarrow can clear the forms without disturbing them.

▶**For smaller pours** that require more accuracy, mix concrete in a mixer, wheelbarrow, or mortar box, and then transfer it to a 5-gal. bucket for delivery. For larger pours, reduce the effect of cold joints by ending the day's work at an expansion joint or control joint.

How to Place Concrete

1 ■ **Load the wheelbarrow** with fresh concrete. Make sure you have a clear path from the source to the site. Always load wheelbarrows from the front; loading wheelbarrows from the side can cause tipping.

2 ■ **Pour concrete in evenly spaced loads** (each load is called a pod). Start at the end farthest from the concrete source, and pour so the top of the pod is a few inches above the top of the forms. Do not pour too close to the forms. Note: If you are using a ramp, stay clear of the end of the ramp.

3 ■ **Continue to place concrete pods** next to preceding pods, working away from the first pod. Do not pour more concrete than you can tool at one time. Keep an eye on the concrete to make sure it does not harden before you can start tooling.

4 ■ **Distribute concrete evenly** in the project area using a masonry hoe. Work the concrete with a hoe until it is fairly flat, and the surface is slightly above the top of the forms. Remove excess concrete with a shovel.

continued next page ▶

How to Place Concrete, continued

5■ **Immediately work** the blade of a spade between the inside edges of the form and the concrete to remove trapped air bubbles that can weaken the concrete.

6■ **Rap the forms with a hammer** or the blade of the shovel to help settle the concrete. This also draws finer aggregates in the concrete against the forms, creating a smoother surface on the sides. This is especially important when building steps.

7■ **Use a screed board**—a straight piece of 2 × 4 long enough to rest on opposite forms—to remove the excess concrete before bleed water appears. Move the screed board in a sawing motion from left to right, and keep the screed flat as you work. If screeding leaves any valleys in the surface, add fresh concrete in the low areas and screed to level.

8■ **Wait until bleed water** disappears (see box, opposite page), then float in an arcing motion with the leading edge of the tool up. Stop floating as soon as the surface is smooth.

9 ■ **Add a nonslip finish** by drawing a clean stiff-bristle broom across the surface once the concrete is thumbprint hard. Make sure all strokes are made in the same direction and avoid overlapping.

10 ■ **Cut control joints** at marked locations with a groover, using a straight 2 x 4 as a guide. Control joints are designed to control where the slab cracks in the future, as natural heaving and settling occur. Without control joints a slab may develop a jagged, disfiguring crack. Control joints must be placed a minimum of ¼ the depth of the slab (1"-deep control joints in a 4" slab).

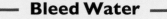

— Bleed Water —

Timing is key to an attractive concrete finish. When concrete is poured, the heavy materials gradually sink, leaving a thin layer of water—known as bleed water—on the surface.

To achieve a durable, attractive finish, it's important to let bleed water dry before proceeding with other steps. Follow these rules to avoid problems:

■ Settle and screed the concrete immediately after pouring and before bleed water appears. Otherwise, crazing, spalling, and other flaws are likely.

■ Let bleed water dry before floating or edging. Concrete should be hard enough that foot pressure leaves no more than a ¼"-deep impression.

■ Note: Less bleed water appears with air-entrained concrete, which is used in regions where temperatures often fall below freezing.

11 ■ **Shape concrete** with an edging tool between the forms and the concrete to create a smooth, finished appearance. You may need to make several passes. Use a wood float to smooth out any marks left by the groover or edger.

12 ■ **Apply acrylic cure** and seal with a garden sprayer or roller to eliminate the need for water curing and to seal the concrete for a more durable surface. ◆

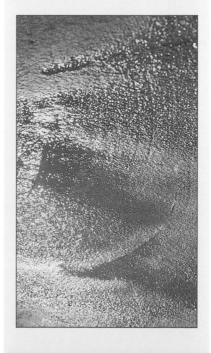

Working with Mortar

Working with brick and block is a satisfying process: with each unit that is added, the project grows and its appearance improves. Whether you're building a block retaining wall, a brick barbeque, or paving a walk with mortared brick, you're sure to enjoy the project as well as its results.

Brick and block provide a sense of balance as well as color and texture to your home and landscape. Structures built with these materials are attractive, durable, and low maintenance.

Careful planning and a thoughtful design will help you build a project that makes sense for your home, your yard, and your budget. Projects are simpler to build if you create a design that limits the number of masonry units that must be cut.

Brick and decorative block colors, styles, and textures vary widely by region, reflecting regional trends. Choose a color and style that complements the style of your home and yard as well as the region in which you live. Colors and styles are often discontinued abruptly, so it's a good idea to buy a few extra units to have on hand for repairs.

QUIK-TIP

Laying brick and block is a precise business. Many of the tools necessary for these projects relate to establishing and maintaining true, square, and level structures, while others relate to cutting the masonry units and placing the mortar. It makes sense to purchase tools you'll use again, but it's more cost effective to rent specialty items, such as a brick splitter.

Tools for Brick and Block Projects

■ **Mason's tools** include a story pole (A) for checking stacked masonry units; masonry hoe (B) and mortar box (C) for mixing mortar; a bucket (D) and stiff bristle brushes (E) for removing stains and loose materials; circular saw and masonry-cutting blades (F) for scoring brick and block; level (G) for checking stacked masonry units; mortar hawk (H) for holding mortar; mortar bag (I) for filling horizontal joints; rubber mallet (J) for setting paver stones; pointing trowel (K) for furrowing mortar; London trowel (L) for applying mortar; brick tongs (M) for carrying multiple bricks; brick sets (N) for splitting brick, block, and stone; cold chisels (O) for scoring masonry units; a tape measure and chalk line (P) for marking layout lines on footings or slabs; a framing square (Q) for setting project outlines; 3/8" dowels (R) for spacers between dry-laid masonry units; mason's string (S) and line blocks (T) for stacking brick and block; a line level (U) for making layouts and setting slope; sled jointer (V) for finishing long joints; mason's hammer (W) for chipping brick and stone; tuck pointer (X); S-shaped jointer (Y); aviation snips (Z) for trimming metal ties and lath; pipe clamps (AA) for aligning brick and block to be scored; caulk gun (BB) for sealing around fasteners and house trim.

■ **Common types of brick and block** used for residential construction include decorative block (A) available colored or plain, decorative concrete pavers (B), fire brick (C), standard 8 × 8 × 16" concrete block (D), half block (E), combination corner block (F), queen-sized brick (G), standard brick pavers (H), standard building bricks (I), and limestone wall cap (J).

Mortar Mixes

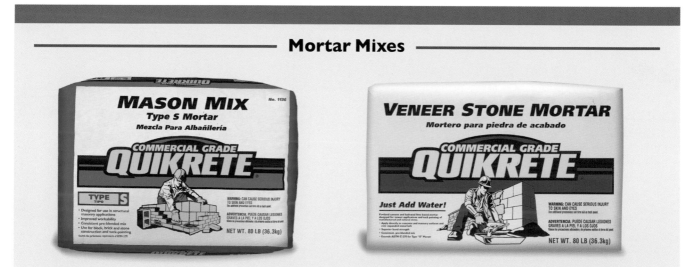

▶**Mortar mixes** include Type N, a medium-strength mortar (750 psi) for above-grade outdoor use in nonload-bearing (freestanding) walls, barbeques, chimneys, and tuck-pointing; Type S, a high-strength mortar (1,800 psi) for outdoor use at or below grade, typically used in foundations, retaining walls, driveways, walks, and patios; and veneer stone mortar, a low-sag, high-bond strength mortar designed for use in veneer stone and natural stone applications.

Tips for Planning a Brick or Block Project

▶**Frost footings are required** if a structure will be more than 2 ft. tall or if it is tied to another permanent structure. Frost footings should be twice as wide as the structure they support and should extend 8 to 12" below the frost line.

▶**Pour a reinforced concrete slab** for brick and block structures that are freestanding and under 2 ft. tall. The slab should be twice as wide as the wall, flush with ground level, and at least 8" thick. Check with building codes for special requirements. Slabs are poured using the techniques for pouring a sidewalk (pages 10 to 15).

▶**Do not add mortar joint thickness** to total project dimensions when planning brick and block projects. The actual sizes of bricks and blocks are $3/8$" smaller than the nominal size to allow for $3/8$"-wide mortar joints. For example, a 9" (nominal) brick has an actual dimension of $8^5/8$", so a wall that is built with four 9" bricks and $3/8$" mortar joints will have a finished length of 36" (4 x 9").

▶**Test project layouts** using $3/8$" spacers between masonry units to make sure the planned dimensions work. If possible, create a plan that uses whole bricks or blocks, reducing the amount of cutting required.

How to Lay Out a Wall

1■ **To get a sense** of the size and impact of a wall or other project before you begin construction, plot the borders of the project using tall stakes or poles, then tie mason's strings marking the projected top of the structure.

2■ **Hang landscape fabric** or sheets of plastic between the stakes and over the top of the string. View the structure from all sides for an indication of how much it will obstruct views and access, and how it will blend with other elements of the landscape. ◆

Working with a Water Level

■ Water levels take advantage of the fact that water in an open tube will level itself, no matter how many bends and turns the tube has. This makes a water level ideal for working with long structures, around corners, or on sites where a conventional level won't work. Typical commercially available water levels consist of clear plastic tubes that screw onto the ends of a garden hose (right, top).

■ Mark off 1" increments on each tube. Attach the tubes to the ends of a garden hose, then fill the hose until water is visible in both tubes. Working with a helper, hold the tubes at the ends of the site. Adjust the tubes until the water is at the same mark in each tube (right, bottom). Drive stakes or mark off the level points on your structure. Option: Pricier water levels contain an electronic gauge that's useful when you need precise readings.

How to Plot Right Angles and Round Corners

1■ The 3-4-5 triangle method is the most effective method of plotting right angles for walls, pillars, and other construction. Begin by staking the outside corner of your walls and stringing a mason's string to mark the outside of one wall.

2■ Mark a point 3 ft. out along that wall by planting another stake.

3■ Position the end of one tape measure at the outside corner and open it past the 4 ft. mark. Have an assistant position the end of another tape measure at the 3 ft. stake and open it past the 5 ft. mark. Lock the tape measures and adjust them so they intersect at the 4 ft. and 5 ft. marks.

4■ Plant a stake at the meeting point, then run mason's strings from this stake to the outside corner. The 3 ft. and 4 ft. mason's strings form a right angle. Extend or shorten the mason's strings, as required, and stake out the exact dimensions of your structure. ◆

Tips for Reinforcing Brick & Block Structure

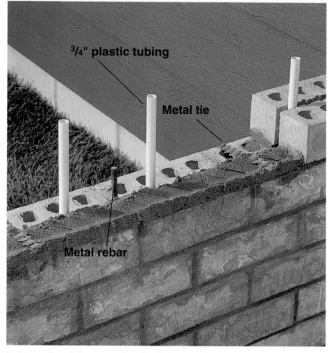

3/4" plastic tubing

Metal tie

Metal rebar

▶**For double-wythe brick projects,** use metal ties between wythes for reinforcement. Insert ties directly into the mortar 2 to 3 ft. apart, every third course. Insert metal rebar into the gap between wythes every 4 to 6 ft. (check local building codes). Insert ¾"- dia. plastic tubing between wythes to keep them aligned. Pour a flowable mixture of concrete mix or sand topping mix between the wythes to improve the strength of the wall.

▶**For block projects,** fill the empty spaces (cores) of the block with sand topping mix or core-fill grout. Insert sections of metal rebar into the mortar to increase vertical strength. Check with your local building inspector to determine reinforcement requirements, if any.

▶**Provide horizontal reinforcement** on brick or block walls by setting metal reinforcing strips into the mortar every third course. Metal reinforcing strips, along with most other reinforcing products, can be purchased from brick and block suppliers. Overlap the ends of metal strips 6" where they meet.

Tips for Working with Brick

▶**Make practice runs** on a 2 × 4 to help you perfect your mortar-throwing and bricklaying techniques. You can clean and reuse the bricks to make many practice runs if you find it helpful, but do not reuse the bricks in your actual project—old mortar can impede bonding.

▶ **Test the water absorption rate** of bricks to determine their density. Squeeze out 20 drops of water in the same spot on the surface of a brick. If the surface is completely dry after 60 seconds, dampen the bricks with water before you lay them to prevent them from absorbing moisture from the mortar before it has a chance to set.

▶ **Use a T-square and pencil** to mark several bricks for cutting. Make sure the ends of the bricks are all aligned.

▶**Mark angled cuts** by dry-laying the project (as shown with pavers above) and setting the brick or block in position. Allow for ³/₈" joints in mortared projects. Pavers have spacing lugs that set the spacing at ¹/₈". Mark cutting lines with a pencil using a straightedge where practical to mark straight lines.

How to Score & Cut Brick

1■ **Score all four sides of the brick** first with a brickset chisel and maul when cuts fall over the web area, and not over the core. Tap the chisel to leave scored cutting marks ⅛ to ¼" deep, then strike a firm final blow to the chisel to split the brick. Properly scored bricks split cleanly with one firm blow.

▶ **Option:** When you need to split a lot of bricks uniformly and quickly, use a circular saw fitted with a masonry blade to score the bricks, then split them individually with a chisel. For quick scoring, clamp them securely at each end with a pipe or bar clamp, making sure the ends are aligned. Remember: wear eye protection when using striking or cutting tools. ◆

How to Angle-cut Brick

Cutting marks

Pivot Point

1■ **Mark the final cutting line** on the brick. To avoid ruining the brick, you will need to make gradual cuts until you reach this line. Score a straight line for the first cut in the waste area of the brick about ⅛" from the starting point of the final cutting line, perpendicular to the edge of the brick. Make the first cut.

2■ **Keep the chisel stationary** at the point of the first cut, pivot it slightly, then score and cut again. It is important to keep the pivot point of the chisel at the edge of the brick. Repeat until all of the waste area is removed. ◆

How to Cut Brick with a Brick Splitter

1▪ **A brick splitter** makes accurate, consistent cuts in bricks and pavers with no scoring required. It is a good idea to rent one if your project requires many cuts. To use the brick splitter, first mark a cutting line on the brick, then set the brick on the table of the splitter, aligning the cutting line with the cutting blade on the tool.

2▪ **Once the brick is in position** on the splitter table, pull down sharply on the handle. The cutting blade on the splitter will cleave the brick along the cutting line. For efficiency, mark cutting lines on several bricks at the same time (see page 151). ◆

How to Cut Concrete Block

1▪ **Mark cutting lines** on both faces of the block, then score ⅛ to ¼"-deep cuts along the lines using a circular saw equipped with a masonry blade.

2▪ **Use a mason's chisel** and maul to split one face of the block along the cutting line. Turn the block over and split the other face.

▶**Option:** Cut half blocks from combination corner blocks. Corner blocks have preformed cores in the center of the web. Score lightly above the core, then rap with a mason's chisel to break off half blocks. ◆

QUIK-DATA

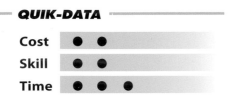

Cost ● ●

Skill ● ●

Time ● ● ●

TOOLS

Trowel, hoe, shovel.

MATERIALS

Mortar mix, mortar box, plywood blocks.

Mixing & Placing Mortar

A professional bricklayer at work is an impressive sight, even for do-it-yourselfers who have completed numerous masonry projects successfully. The mortar practically flies off the trowel and seems to end up in perfect position to accept the next brick or block. Although "throwing mortar" is an acquired skill that takes years to perfect, you can use the basic techniques successfully with just a little practice. The first critical element to handling mortar effectively is the mixture. If it's too thick, it will fall off the trowel in a heap, not in the smooth line that is your goal. Add too much water and the mortar becomes messy and weak. Follow the manufacturer's directions, but keep in mind that the amount of water specified is an approximation. If you've never mixed mortar before, experiment with small amounts until you find a mixture that clings to the trowel just long enough for you to deliver a controlled, even line that holds its shape after settling. Note how much water you use in each batch, and record the best mixture. Mix mortar for a large project in batches; on a hot, dry day a large batch will harden before you know it. If mortar begins to thicken, add water (called retempering); use retempered mortar within two hours.

Tips for Working with Mortar

◆**Remove wet mortar** from joints in natural stone walls using a jointer or even piece of wood. By raking out ½" or so of mortar you will create a wall with subtle shadow lines between stones instead of tooled mortar, which can look a bit out of place with irregular stone.

◆**Blend liquid stucco and mortar pigment** with the mixing water before adding to the dry mortar mix. Add the same amount of color and water to each batch for color consistency.

How to Mix & Place Mortar

1 ■ **Empty mortar mix** into a mortar box and form a depression in the center. Add about ¾ of the recommended amount of water into the depression, then mix it in with a masonry hoe. Do not overwork the mortar. Continue adding small amounts of water and mixing until the mortar reaches the proper consistency. Do not mix too much mortar at one time—mortar is much easier to work with when it is fresh.

2 ■ **Set a piece of plywood** on blocks at a convenient height, and place a shovelful of mortar onto the surface. Slice off a strip of mortar from the pile using the edge of your mason's trowel. Slip the trowel point-first under the section of mortar and lift up.

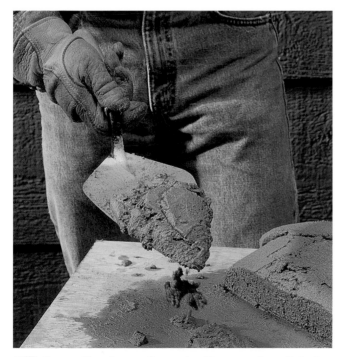

3 ■ **Snap the trowel** gently downward to dislodge excess mortar clinging to the edges. Position the trowel at the starting point, and place a line of mortar onto the building surface. A good amount is enough to set three bricks. Do not get ahead of yourself. If you place too much mortar, it will set before you are ready.

4 ■ **"Furrow"** the mortar line by dragging the point of the trowel through the center of the mortar line in a slight back-and-forth motion. Furrowing helps distribute the mortar evenly. ◆

Glossary

A

Adhesion The sticking together of substances that are in contact with one another.

Admixtures All materials, other than Portland cement, water, and aggregates, that are added to concrete, mortar, or grout immediately before or during mixing.

Aggregate Bulk materials, such as sand, gravel, crushed stone, slag, pumice, and scoria, that are used in making concrete.

Anchor Bolts Any of a variety of rather large J- or L-shaped bolts designed to have a portion embedded in concrete or mortar.

Ashlars A squared or rectangular block of building stones in the ashlar pattern.

B

Backfilling The process of piling earth against the outer surface of a form.

Base Coat Each of the lower layers of plaster, if more than one coat is applied.

Batter Boards A board frame supported by stakes set back from the corners of a structure that allows for relocating certain points after excavation. Saw kerfs in the boards indicate the location of the edges of the footings and the structure being built.

Bed Joint The horizontal layer of mortar on which a masonry unit is laid.

Block A concrete masonry unit made with fine aggregate and cement that is shaped in a mold. Any of a variety of shaped lightweight or standard-weight masonry units.

Bond The property of a hardened mortar that knits the masonry units together; also the lapping of brick in a wall.

Brick Masonry A type of construction that has units of baked clay or shale of uniform size, small enough to be placed with one hand, laid in courses with mortar joints to form walls of virtually unlimited length and height.

Brick Set A wide-blade chisel used for cutting bricks and concrete blocks.

Brown Coat Second coat of plaster or stucco in three-coat work.

Buttered The small end of a brick that has quantity of mortar placed onto it (e.g., the act of buttering a brick's end with mortar).

C

Caulk To seal up crevices with some flexible material.

Closure Brick A partial brick that is cut to fit into place to complete a course.

Coloring Agents Colored aggregates or mineral oxides ground finer than cement.

Concrete An artificial stone made by mixing cement and sand with gravel, broken stone, or other aggregate. These materials must be mixed with sufficient water to cause the cement to set and bind the entire mass.

Control Joints A cut or score at least ¼ of element depth designed to direct where cracks occur.

Coping A brick, block, stone, or concrete cap placed at the top of a masonry wall to prevent moisture from falling directly on it and weakening the wall.

Corbeling Courses of bricks set out beyond the face of a wall in order to form a self-supporting projection.

Courses One of the continuous horizontal layers (rows) of masonry that forms the masonry structure.

Curing The process of protecting concrete against loss of moisture during the earliest stage of setting.

D

Dry Mixture Mixture of concrete whose water content is severely restricted.

E

Edger A concrete finishing tool for rounding the edge of freshly poured concrete; one of several finishing techniques.

Edging The process of rounding the edge of freshly poured concrete; one of several finishing techniques.

Efflorescence A powdery stain, usually white, on the surface of or between masonry units. It is caused by the leaching of soluble salts to the surface.

Expansion Joint A space between a concrete slab or wall and another building element which allows for thermal expansion and contraction without cracking. Almost always filled with a flexible material.

Exposed Aggregate

Exposed Aggregate A concrete finish achieved by embedding aggregate into the surface, allowing the concrete to set up somewhat, then hosing down and brushing away the concrete covering the top portion of the aggregate.

F

Face Brick A type of brick made specifically for covering (veneering) walls.

Finish Coat The top layer of plaster if the plaster is applied in more than one coat.

Flashing The waterproofing covering placed to set up certain points in brick masonry to hold water or to direct any moisture outside the wall.

Float A wooden tool used to finish a concrete surface.

Footing A base for a wall or structure that provides stability for that structure.

Form A parameter or set of parameters made from earth or wood and, on occasion, steel, that contains the footage concrete.

Frost Line The maximum depth to which frost normally penetrates the soil during the winter. This depth varies from area to area depending on the climate.

Furrowing Striking a V-shaped trough in a bed of mortar.

G

Gradation The distribution of particle sizes, from coarse to fine, in a given sample of fine or coarse aggregate.

Grout A water-cement or water-cement-sand mixture used to plug holes or cracks in concrete, seal joints, fill spaces between machinery bed plates and concrete foundations, and for similar plugging or sealing purposes.

H

Hawk A fairly small board with a handle beneath it used for holding mortar.

Header A masonry unit laid flat with its longest dimensions perpendicular to the face of the wall. It is generally used to tie two wythes of masonry together.

Hydration The chemical reaction that occurs when water is added to cement, causing it to harden.

J

Joint Any place where two or more edges or surfaces come to a union.

Jointer A tool used for making grooves or control joints in concrete surfaces to control cracking (see Control Joints).

Joist In deck construction, 2 x 6" lumber attached to beams and ledgers that serves as a base for the deck planking.

L

Lintel A beam placed over an opening in a wall.

M

Masonry A construction made of prefabricated masonry units laid in various ways and joined together with mortar.

Mixers Vehicles or containers used to blend or mix the ingredients of concrete.

Moisture Content The amount of water contained within the aggregate used in concrete.

Mortar A mixture of cement, sand, and water without coarse aggregate. It is used chiefly for bonding masonry units together.

P

Pavers Bricks in numerous sizes and shapes that are used in constructing sidewalks, patios, and driveways.

Pier A free-standing column.

Pilaster A projection from a masonry wall that provides strength for the wall.

Plastic Consistency A sluggish flow without segregation.

Plumb That which is vertically perpendicular as measured with a spirit level or plumb bob.

Pointing The process of inserting mortar into horizontal and vertical joints after a masonry unit is laid.

Portland Cement A number of types of cement with unique characteristics manufactured from limestone and mixed with shale, clay, or marl.

Precast Concrete Any concrete member that is cast in forms at a place other than its final position of use.

Premix Any of several packaged mixtures of ingredients used for preparing concrete or mortar.

R

Reinforcing Rod A steel rod that is used for reinforcing concrete and masonry structures.

Retaining Wall
A wall that is constructed to hold soil in place.

Rowlock
A brick laid on its edge (face).

Rubble Rough fragments of broken stone either naturally formed or quarried; used in masonry.

Running Bond This is the same as common bond with continuous horizontal joints, but the vertical joints are offset or in line.

S

Scratch Coat The first coat of plaster or stucco.

Screed A long, very straight board used for striking off concrete.

Screeding The process of leveling the surface of a concrete slab by striking off the excess concrete.

Segregation The tendency of particles of the same size in a given mass of aggregate to gather together whenever the material is being loaded, transported, or otherwise disturbed.

Set The process during which mortar or concrete hardens. Initial set occurs when the concrete has to be broken to change its shapes, generally about an hour after it is placed. Final set occurs generally about 10 hours after placing the concrete.

Shell The sides and recessed ends of a concrete block.

Soldier A brick laid on its ends so that its longest dimension is parallel to the vertical axis of the face of the wall.

Stretcher A masonry unit laid flat with its longest dimension parallel to the face of the wall.

Striking Off The process of removing excess concrete to a level needed.

Stucco A finish composed of two or more layers of mortar (white or colored) that is applied to either indoor or outdoor walls.

T

Tamp The process of compacting concrete with rakes or short lengths of lumber.

Texturizing Creating a particular finish, such as brushed, smoothed, etched, or pockmarked.

Ties A wire, rod, or snap that is used to hold wall forms at a specific separation.

Trowel A steel tool with a flat surface that causes a concrete surface to become very smooth.

Tuck-Pointing The process of refilling old joints with new mortar.

V

Veneer A layer of bricks or stones that serves as a facing.

W

Wales Horizontal members that aid in wall/form reinforcement and distribution of forces.

Weep Holes The openings made in mortar joints that facilitate drainage of built-up moisture.

Wire Mesh Any of a variety of types of bonded wire forming a mat used to reinforce slabs of concrete.

Workability The ease or difficulty of placing and consolidating concrete.

Wythe A vertical stack of bricks one thickness wide (e.g., a veneer course).

Metric Conversion Chart

Metric Conversions

To Convert:	To:	Multiply by:
Inches	Millimeters	25.4
Inches	Centimeters	2.54
Feet	Meters	0.305
Yards	Meters	0.914
Square inches	Square centimeters	6.45
Square feet	Square meters	0.093
Square yards	Square meters	0.836
Ounces	Milliliters	29.6
Pints (U.S.)	Liters	0.473 (Imp. 0.568)
Quarts (U.S.)	Liters	0.946 (Imp. 1.136)
Gallons (U.S.)	Liters	3.785 (Imp. 4.546)
Ounces	Grams	28.4
Pounds	Kilograms	0.454

To Convert:	To:	Multiply by:
Millimeters	Inches	0.039
Centimeters	Inches	0.394
Meters	Feet	3.28
Meters	Yards	1.09
Square centimeters	Square inches	0.155
Square meters	Square feet	10.8
Square meters	Square yards	1.2
Milliliters	Ounces	.034
Liters	Pints (U.S.)	2.114 (Imp. 1.76)
Liters	Quarts (U.S.)	1.057 (Imp. 0.88)
Liters	Gallons (U.S.)	0.264 (Imp. 0.22)
Grams	Ounces	0.035
Kilograms	Pounds	2.2

Photo Credits

p. 7 photo © Jessie Walker

p. 8 photo © Wayne Howard / www.istock.com

p. 9 photo (top right) Estudio Arqué Design, photo by Andrea Maggi, (middle) Becker Architectural Concrete, (lower right) istock / www.istock.com

p. 35 photo © Clive Nichols, designer Jennifer Hirsch

p. 36 photo courtesy of U-Line

p. 37 photo (top left) © Robert Agli, photo (middle) © Clive Nichols

p. 63 photo © Clive Nichols

p. 64 photo © Beth Singer

p. 65 photos (all) © Clive Nichols, (top) designer Christopher Bradley-Hole, (top, right) designer Amir Schlezinger/ My Landscapes, (middle) designer Elizabeth Apedaite/Dove Landscapes

p. 66 photo courtesy of Cultured Stone Corporation

p. 70 photo © Beth Singer

p. 90 photo © Clive Nichols, designer Jane Mooney

p. 97 photo © Simone Paddock

p. 106 photo courtesy of Seattle Glass Block

p. 112 photo © Simone Paddock

Contact Information

Becker Architectural Concrete
651 554 0346
www.beckerconcrete.com

Cultured Stone Corporation
800 255 1727
www.culturedstone.com

Estudio Arqué
+ 34 956 695 896 – 690 656 675
email: info@estudioarque.com
www.estudioarque.com

Seattle Glass Block
425 483 9977
www.seattleglassblock.com

U-Line
414 354 0300
www.u-line.com

Index